GETTING UNST

M000013978

Oh God, How Could It Be
That I caught HIV
From my Cousin, Justeen?
What's worse This, or Gangrene?
Girl to Girl, You can Be
Infected Indeed...
I Got caught out There's, a fact
Sniffin coke, Dealing crack
Flippin Dough, Buyin weight
Wanna stop, Its too late
I Set up shop, At Grandma's house
Rented rooms, Sold girls out
Smoke right here, Have some fun
Drink some Rum, Even cum
Watch my gun, Watch my back
Someone will, Try attack
I Feel alone, Deep inside
Time to Run, Time to hide
Drug Lords Coming, I Can't wait
To the back, Hop the gate
Learned the yards, Since a kid
Playing tag's, Where I hid
Now I'm bigger, Gotta hide
From Cartels, Glocks, and pride
Stole their Package, and their gun
I'm so slick, I Gotta run
Hide out house, Across the street
I Split the drugs, With Monique
Running scared, I Take a cab
What I need, Is Rehab
Start to think, As I smoke
That this crack, Ain't no joke
That this life, Of today
Could be Death, If I stay
Help me finish, with these drugs
And surrender, Up above
To A voice, Heard in bed
Told me go, Les I'm dead
Said to work, For Me please
That I would, Have disease
Don't you Worry, Go now run
No affect, Til Work's done

Went to groups, Had mad fear
Of these strangers, Up in here
Counselor Allan, Was his name
And his groups, Pulled my pain
Gave me hope, Gave me drive
That my Dream's, Still alive
To one day, I'd become
Someone famous, Not a bum
Allan helped me, Find out
A big secret, no doubt
Repressed Memory
Was the Source!
Found my purpose, and my
thoughts
Changed my life, Got a job
No more people, Did I rob
Life made sense, Hungry now
For success, I will growl
Had a friend, Hit the top
With Mad albums, And big props
Queen Latifah, was Her name
Rapping big, got Her fame
Life had plan, Not a scam
In her studio I would land
All cleaned up, Trusted face
With a job, I got laced
Hard work, and Great soul
Got audition, for a New show
It is here, in my prime
I Work for Oprah, That's part time
God's Work, I will do
Wrote a book, Just for you
Oh God, How Could It Be
Got a Job, on TV
No More Coke,
No More Weed
And I'm Still HIV?

1

Copyright © 1999 by Conscious

All rights reserved, including the right to reproduce this work in any form whatsoever, without permission in writing from the author, except for brief passages in connection with review.

Cover Layout by Starr Graphics (718) 469-6763
Cover Layout by Alexandra De La Cruz / Ryan Paul
Website design by Madison the Promoter (718) 369-6254
Edited by Rachelle Christie
and Elizabeth Otero

For information write
SWN Publishing
PO Box 1133
Union NJ 07083-1133

Or call: 1 (866) 782-2002
E-mail: **conscious@prettytomboys.com**
Website: **www.prettytomboys.com**

If you are unable to order this book from your local bookseller, you may order directly from the publisher. Quantity discounts for organizations are available. Call 1 (866) 782-2002

ISBN # 0-9716951-0-5

Library of Congress Control # 2001119773
Printed in the United States of America

Getting

UNSTUCK

Girl to Girl, You Can Be, Infected Indeed. . ..

By Conscious

SWN Publishing
New Jersey

Deadications

This book is **dead**icated to all of the children who are enduring the pains of sexual abuse and are having a hard time telling someone. Be brave, and tell.

And to the Parents;
Do you know what happens to your kids after you leave?

And to the Abusers;
Please **stop** touching the children. You are making monsters and **dead**ening their innocent souls. Get some help.

And to Peaches;
I will never forget when you took care of me when my back was infected with shingles. I love you.

And to my little boy Anthony;
May you never have to bare witness to a childhood such as mine. I will protect you.

And to my sister, who always understood me, I love you.

And to my little brother, I know your pain but you have to move on. I love you.

And to Mike, who rescued me several times, I love you.

And to my mom, thank you for life, maybe one day we will see eye to eye.

And finally, to my cousin, who **Died** of AIDS.
"I'll see you at the crossroads, you won't be lonely"

All names in this book have been changed to protect the **Guilty**...

Getting Unstuck

i

It was Christmas time and that meant the children could visit. I didn't want to hear that, though. Children make me nervous, especially little girls. Damn, what did I go and say that for? But they wanted to know everything right? So there, I finally said it. What's wrong with me?

Some of the men and women who'd gotten to know and respect me during my first seven months in this drug treatment program started to back off. They began to say nasty things such as, "Don't come near my kids when they come to visit. You're hiding something, and you're guilty of something. Write your guilt down on paper." I was deeply hurt because I never had and never would hurt a child. But something was eating at me.

"You got guilt, Conscious, You got guilt," they said pointing at me, first one person, then another going around the circle.

We were all self-enrolled in Daytop Village, a long-term drug treatment facility in Parksville, New York, during a group session in the dining room. The place was only about three hours north of New York City, my birthplace, but it was like a universe away.

As I sat slouched in my chair with my head down, embarrassed by my secrets, my light-skinned face, grimacing with pain turned beet red and my eyes became puffed from crying out my torment. When I leaned forward my body jerked hard with each cry, as snot bubbled out my nose and mixed with long thick clear spit that dripped down my face to my shirt. My counselor Allan asked me over and over again,

> *What secrets are you holding*
> *back? Tell me all your secrets.*
> *It's the only way you are going*
> *to get well.*

I had been in Allan's care at Daytop for seven months and thought that I was coming near the end of spilling my guts to strangers during these group sessions. Allan was my counselor, but had become my confidant. I had told him everything I could remember about my past, and me.

The Daytop program was a therapeutic community, which had structure, just like the military. There were 175 ex-dope addicts, ex-crack heads, and ex-alcoholics housed in two huge facilities. One facility was for the women and the other for men. The third facility was the main house also known as the Pinnacle. That's where we attended our morning meetings, listened to seminars, ate meals, visited our counselor's office, visited the nurse's office and received new inductees and mail.

The chain of command ranged from the director of the facility down to the newest members in the house, with at least 20 counselors who lived off the grounds. The new residents worked in the cleaning department and kept the Pinnacle spotless while the older residents acted as expeditors who tended to the Pinnacle's daily business; such as accepting deliveries, organizing groups, and manning the telephones. The residents cared for the grounds, prepared the meals, and stood guard overnight. As we followed our program to recovery and remained sober, we moved up in the house. There was no outside help from civilians and no civilians were allowed on the property without a pass, except for the cook who was also a recovering addict. Group meetings with our peers and our counselors were sometimes held outside under a tree on the lawn or in the dinning room in the Pinnacle.

Located on another part of the grounds, was a small building with art classes and activities to help us release our pain. There was a one million-dollar gym facility donated by the alumni for exercise and support from counselors who cared.

Allan was the one assigned to be my counselor. Everybody wanted him to be their counselor because he was so smart and his lectures had us looking for him afterward to hear him speak some more. Allan stimulated our minds and used words that had us referring to a dictionary. He was a 6-feet-4 inches, slim, handsome brown-skinned man who resembled the actor Richard Roundtree. He was strong and arrogant, and I liked that. With frustration in his voice though, he was still asking,

> *What else aren't you telling us? You say all the right things and you seem like you're ready to face the world again, but I know it's not all out. There's something else locked inside. I just know it.*

As the session ended Allan headed upstairs to his office. Meanwhile, the members of the group all got up with their folded chairs clutched under their arms and filed out of the dining room. Without looking up I could see the glares of confusion on their faces, but nothing was more confusing than what was stirring inside of me.

Today was my scheduled one-on-one appointment with Allan right after group and damn, he had me right where he wanted me, too. His invasive series of questions about my deepest secrets had me wide open with my emotions flowing. Once we got upstairs to his office it wouldn't take much more for him to pry out the rest. I just wanted to say,

Stop it Allan, what the hell else do you want from me?

Allan knew there was more to me because, in his professional and personal life, he had been there. His office at Daytop was about the size of a small Burger King rest room. Shoved under a window, there was a bookcase stuffed with sociology, and psychology books. I think they were there for show, because there was a thick layer of dust on them, besides that Allan had so much life experience and intuition that he didn't need to read no psychology books. Better looking, though, were the photographs he displayed of his wife, parents and some of his friends, with their big Sesame Street grins.

On one wall all by itself, was a picture of a man. He was so thin you could see his cheekbones prominent even under and around a scruffy beard. His hair was mangy and he looked so dirty you could practically smell the image. The image looked familiar though, like so many images of men I had seen around my way that were all cracked-out from smoking cocaine. Images of men that had done so many drugs that they forgot about looking good, clean and healthy. From my experience I noticed that when people slip, and allow themselves to reach that point, they don't care about their appearance, themselves, their families, their health, or anything around them. Their only concern is to rush up and down the streets of Harlem to wash windshields and collect enough cans to hustle enough money to get high. It's a wonder that this dude even took the time to pose for the camera. But someone had caught him on film, and Allan had hung this guy's photograph amongst his family and other loved ones as a reminder, to any of us who entered into his care, what drugs could do to a person. Allan knew, because he was that guy in the photograph.

What I disclosed during the group session in the dining room was that I had recalled an awkward moment, with my niece. My older sister, her 6-year-old daughter and I had gone to see a movie. Afterward, we all had to use the ladies' room, but the little one most of all. The ladies' room was flooded with women talking about the movie and moving back and forth between the stalls and the sinks. You could hear women asking for toilet tissue and see toilet tissue being passed under the stalls. When it was our turn, my sister asked me to take my niece in and hold her over the toilet so that she wouldn't touch the dirty public seat, while she herself went into a stall, three doors down. It was a small thing to ask of me, but it quickly became the biggest public dilemma I'd ever experienced. I couldn't do it. I was terrified. I could not reach down and pull this child's pants down. I made her do it herself. Then, I picked her up and held her over the seat, but I was so uncomfortable and tense about doing so that she peed all over the place. I put her down, stepped back and then, couldn't bear to touch her to clean up the mess. By now my sister was standing at our stall saying, "Move out the way. You still don't know how to handle kids. Move!" I was so embarrassed that I backed out of the stall and left the bathroom in a hurry. I could not handle it. I never could handle seeing them naked or bathing them. I was just so uncomfortable and disturbed. And nobody knew my secret. Huh, and me, I never understood it.

Allan taught us during groups and seminars that secrets create psychological blockage and prevent people from growing emotionally. He said that when you are abused at a young age, if left untreated, you remain stuck at that age emotionally and become secretive. Allan said that unshared secrets are guilt, and they make you hide your true feelings about all kinds of things. As a result, we sometimes turn to drugs, alcohol, and other behaviors as a way of acting out and masking the pain and embarrassment that lives within each one of us. I accepted this as truth and I wanted to get well so, up until that day I had written all of my guilt down on paper and shared all of my secrets with the group except that one, and Allan knew all along that I was holding something back. He was right, there was more.

In his office, Allan had a small wooden desk filled with folders and yellow legal pads. There were pens and pencils neatly standing in a holder, a little lamp in the left-hand corner of the desk, a pack of Newports, and an ashtray. There was a brown wooden chair that sat opposite his. That was the seat I sat in every week for the last seven months during our one-on-one sessions, spilling my guts and trying to get better. That was the chair that supported me through all of our conversations. That chair absorbed all of my tears and felt all of my trembles as I cried.

As I sat down Allan took his seat and lit up a cigarette. His office was extremely quiet except for the gasps of air that I took between each sniffle. Knowing that he was on to something during the group session in the dining room, the first question he asked me was,

Were you afraid that you would molest your niece?

Teary-eyed unable to look at him, I said,

No, that's not it.

The thought itself turned my stomach. Then I thought to myself,

Oh no, I hope he don't think I'm no molester, only those sick psychos do that. That shit is sick.

*So, what is it? What would
prevent you from bathing your
nieces, or wiping them with
tissue?*

**I don't know Allan I just have always felt funny
about seeing a kid's vagina or having to clean it.**

*Well what happened to you
when you were a little girl, did
someone touch your vagina?*

No. I don't think so. I don't know.

Confused, I just shrugged my shoulders not making
full sense of what Allan was getting at. No one had ever
asked me that question. Hell, I had never asked myself that
question.

*Sit back in your chair and tell
me about when you were little
Conscious. Think about when
you were about 7-years old.*

*Can you remember the house
you were in?*

Uh huh, I used to have to stay at my cousin's house a lot.

Why, where was your mother?

She used to make a lot of money hustling. Afterwards, she hung out in the after-hours spots and the bars on the "Ave," but before she did all of that she took me, my brothers and my sister to my cousins house down on Broadway.

Ok, who was in the house?

My aunts, cousins, and friends of the family. There was a lot of us.

About how many?

About sixteen of us.

Can you see the bedrooms,
where did you sleep, how did
your pillow smell?

Yeah I can see the bedrooms, and the pillows. The pillows smelled funky, especially the beds and the pillows in my Aunts room. She was about seventy years old and her room smelled like an old folks-home. Every mattress in the house smelled pissy, and under the sheets we slept on there were plastic bags to prevent the piss from seeping through to the mattress when the kids peed the bed. But it didn't matter though, because the sheets never got changed. The sheets always smelled like piss. There was piss all over my clothes because all of the babies and the little kids slept together.

Who were the adults there?
What were they doing?

Well my Aunt Cookie, she was a dope addict. It seemed as though she used to nod out every time the song "Me and Mrs. Jones" would come on. She used to come in the bathroom while I was sitting on

16

the toilet, roll up her sleeve, rap a big rubberband around her arm and then shoot dope. Then she would sing out loud "Meeee and myyyyyyy, Mrs., Mrs. Jonessssssss. Mrs. Jones, Mrs. Jones, Mrs. Jones, " while she would nod towards the toilet and then abruptly stand back up before she fell on me.

Did she ever try to touch you while you were in the bathroom?

No Aunt Cookie was cool she just shot her dope and cussed everybody out for going in and out of the house at all hours of the night.

What other things went on in the house?

Well most of the times while the adults were in the front room, my boy cousins and girl cousins were humping each other and having sex in the back room's closet or kissing under the beds. While all of that was going on my cousin Gerald, the "girl child," and me, set one of the mattresses on fire and climbed out the back room window. We tied knots in the sheets and connected the last one to the radiator by the window so we could escape. After Aunt Cookie put the fire out with pots filled with water, she found us outside playing tag and beat us up and down the street with her belt.

Why did you call your cousin Gerald a "girl child?"

We all called him that, mainly because he was so feminine. We all thought that he must have been gay from the day he was born, besides, my cousin Belinda used to tell me and Gerald, that he was the girl and that I was the boy, because he was so feminine and I was so masculine.

What did the backroom look like? How did it smell?

The backroom was funky with three twin beds that had clothes all over them. There was also one single bed, and a cot that sat folded up in the corner. The walls were dingy white and the light bulb in the ceiling was always dim. The lower parts of the walls were full of crayon scribble from the little kids and the upper parts of the walls were full of pen writing by the teenagers. The ceiling was old with peeling paint that was constantly falling on the floor, and the floor was old, dirty and wooden, with splinters that pierced our little feet when we walked. We constantly had to pick the splinters out with a diaper pin after we burned it with a match. Over in the corner by the two windows that were covered by filthy white metal venetian blinds was a pile of smelly dirty clothes and dirty diapers. The clothes were literally stacked to the ceiling, but they came in handy as a hiding place when we played hide-and-go seek.

Where did you eat?

Sometimes we ate in the kitchen that was infested with roaches and mice running under the table. When we turned the light on in the kitchen we had to keep half of our body and our feet outside the door while we reached in to flip the switch.

Why?

To give the mice and the roaches a chance to clear out. We wanted to make sure they didn't fly down from the ceiling into our hair or crawl up our legs. More than any thing, we didn't want to step on them. It didn't matter what we did though because when we opened the refrigerator there they were again, waiting inside to greet us. And when we wanted to make toast, we had to turn the toaster on first and then put the bread in after the roaches ran out of the hot slots.

It was gross huh?

Yeah, but when you are hungry and all the adults are either high from shooting dope or running in the house and out the back room window to escape the cops, you fend for yourself and get your food the best way you can. You feed yourself no matter what you have to go through to get the food. That includes fighting the mice and the roaches.

When Aunt Cookie was busy
who watched you?

My cousin Belinda.

What was Belinda like?

Belinda was a mean, nappy headed child that always had seizures. She had seizures so bad, that we used to have to put a spoon on top of her tongue in order to prevent her from swallowing it. If she wasn't having a seizure then she was doing something bad for attention, or making me do things to her.

Things like what?

Like one time, to get attention from Aunt Cookie, Belinda told me to take to lampshade off a lit lamp and put the hot bulb on her leg, so that it would burn her.

And did you do it?

Yes and when I did it she screamed and told Aunt Cookie that I burned her with the lamp so that I could get in trouble.

Did you bathe?

Sometimes.

Who bathed you when it was
time for bed?

When we did take a bath, which was rare, Belinda bathed Gerald and me in the bath together.

Did anyone else ever touch
you in the bathroom?

I paused before I answered and then let out a shriek that could be heard halfway back to New York.

Yes, oh my God Allan.

What Conscious, what?

Yeah, they used to touch me in the bathroom and then lay me and Gerald down on our stomachs and stuff the tissue, the nasty tissue.

Who?

I didn't want to think about what was pouring into my mind. My eyes started to race around the room, and as I grabbed on to the arms of the chair I shook my head and began to scream no, no, no! I wanted to stop the session because the memories, the smell, the bathroom, the toilet paper, the pissy bedrooms and my cousins. It all began to come back to me.

I jumped up and started screaming and slamming all the stuff off Allan's desk. I felt so much pain that I began to pound the walls. I couldn't believe this had happened to me. I cried, hollered, kicked and jumped up and down. Allan tried to subdue me but I fought him off.

Get off of me!

I was lashing out at everyone and everything that I remembered, but I couldn't touch them. It was all too long ago.

Allan had finally stimulated that part of my brain that had forgotten, and God had allowed me for the first time in more than 20 years to remember filthy memories of my past. Filthy memories that had poured into my mind as if a garbage truck had just poured the day's trash into a dumpsite.

2

*Now tell me, when did it all
begin Conscious? Where did
all of the chaos begin?*

I paused for a moment then said slowly.

**It started in my home with my mom when I was
about six.**

I was numb as I sat in my chair with my elbows on my
knees. My hands supported my face as I looked down to the
floor in a daze. I tried to get myself together enough to look at
Allan, but my hands kept shaking and my voice kept
quivering. My new revelation had catapulted me so far back
into my childhood that I faded far away from Allan. I needed
that time to "space out" though, and piece my life together.
After I went over everything in my mind I became focused
and began to fade back to Allan. I was back in Allan's office,
and now I was angry.

Are you ready Conscious?

Yes.

*Then go as far back as you
can go.*

Ok.

Where did you live?

**We lived north of Harlem in an area known as Sugar
Hill or Washington Heights, a place where peoples'
lives depended on the underground illegal economy.
By the time I was born in 1965, my mom was in her
mid-20's with two other children, my eldest brother
and my sister. She would have one other child five
years after me, my little brother. We all had different
fathers, but we didn't think much about that aside
from the fact that I was much lighter in skin color
than the rest of them and had a hair texture that
was lighter in color and curlier. This set me apart
from them, mostly because they teased me about it.
They called me "the yellow banana."**

What was your mother like,
what did she do for a living?

My mom was off the hook. She was a gangster, a shot caller and everyone feared her, even me, because of her volatile temper.

My mother was a lively, beautiful, stylish, brown-skinned woman. She was the loudest thing on the block. She was a "Baller" in the fast track, pushing a two-seater Mercedes-Benz, wearing mink coats and flashy diamonds. Her wrists jiggled with Cartier watches, and 24 karat gold bracelets. She sported Louis Vuitton pocket books, long wigs, leather pants, and flashed plenty of cash wherever she went. She was outspoken, and women as well as men jumped when she said jump. She was hooked up with a couple of the money-getting dope dealers, and number runners uptown. They called her "Fighting Coffee Brown" and they all adored her company because she was a bad ass that didn't take any shit. Besides that, she did them lots of favors, delivered packages, collected money, and set up meetings for them. In return she got a piece of the action, which kept plenty of money in her pockets and in the safe under her bed. She had a reputation, not only for being smart and stylish, but for not tolerating anyone who "messed with the family." Her favorite saying was "If you don't take care of your business honey, then your business will take care of you."

Her vanity at home was stacked with the best perfumes and her clothes racks were filled with expensive clothes minks and footwear. She shopped at Tiffany's, Sak's Fifth Avenue, Lord and Taylor, and Bergdorf Goodman and she was full of herself. There were mirrors on her headboard, on the ceilings in her bedroom, the backs of all the doors, and on all the walls in the apartment. She drank the finest wines and cognacs and especially liked champagne. There was always a bottle next to her bed on the nightstand.

Where was your father Conscious?

Oh my father, I never got a chance to spend time with him.

Why not?

Because my parents broke up when I was younger. My father probably wasn't down with all that shit my mother was into, who knows. She never told me why they broke up nor would she talk about my father. All I knew was that his mother was white.

Ironically, my mother conceived me with my father who was a big handsome New York City Police Officer named Goldstein. My mother did not marry my father because the gap between their two worlds became wider and wider in the short time that they were together. Eventually they split up when I was 6. The next time I saw him he was dead.

*Tell me about your mother and
how she grew up as a child.
What were her values? Who
did she look up to?*

Well, there was Aunt Beatrice, my mom's father, her second-generation cousins who lived down on Henry Street, and then there was an old great aunt named Regina who lived down on Broadway. Aunt

Regina took care of all of Aunt Cookie's kids, grandkids, my brothers, and sister when our parents weren't around.

My mother's father was a World War I veteran who came home and became a number's runner in Harlem. Her mother was a talented showgirl who died when my mother was a child. Between Granddad and Aunt Beatrice, mom had a lavish childhood with the best clothes, a cleaning lady and the opportunity to obtain a good education.

Tell me about this Aunt Beatrice, do you remember her apartment or the things that went on there.

Yeah, but only a little because I was really young then.

Ok, go on, tell me what you remember.

Aunt Beatrice's apartment was spotless with old antique furniture and old lamps. Her apartment was located on the fifth floor of this well-kept building with a doorman on St. Nicholas Avenue, where she raised my mother as her own.

Her closets were full of mink coats, alligator shoes, priceless dresses and big round hats that she kept in boxes. Her jewelry that was passed down from generation to generation was kept in a safe, with plenty of cash in her closet. She brought in enough money, playing numbers and gambling, to keep my mother in mink coats and elaborate jewelry, too. My mom wanted for nothing.

Aunt Betty's environment was lively. She was a flashy-dressing, fast-talking, sassy old lady in her 60's. She was short thin woman with a few wrinkles on her face. She was a classy old lady who kept a martini glass in one hand and a cigarette propped in the other. Aunt Beatrice was well-liked amongst her peers because she kept scheduled card games and parties going on in her apartment. On card nights the dining room was filled with smoke from cigars and cigarettes. From my bedroom I could hear the cling of ice and the clang of bottles of Johnny Walker Red and Tanqueray hitting each glass as she served them. There were decks of cards, chips, ashtrays, and coasters on the table surrounded by folding chairs. There were old men and women all dressed up and talking on different sides of the room before the card game began. I was supposed to be sleeping but I sat on the floor of my bedroom door and absorbed it all until I fell asleep right there.

Did she ever touch you in a sexual way?

No, it wasn't her. She was into all of her materialistic stuff and her men friends.

Well what ever became of your aunt?

Aunt Betty had a stroke one year and never quite recovered. She had to walk with a cane so she couldn't host her gambling parties like before. Later that year when she and I were alone she had collapsed on the bedroom floor and wouldn't get up. I tried to give her a cane to get up, but she just lay there. I shouted to her "Get up, Aunt Betty, get up" and then the telephone rang. I tried to get her to answer it, but she would not move.

Was she dead?

Uh huh.

My aunt from the projects down on Henry Street was on the phone. She said "Conscious where is Aunt Betty?" I said, "Right here, she's laying on the floor." "Put her on the phone." I tried to put the phone to Aunt Betty's ear but she would not talk. Innocently I said, "She don't want to talk to you." My aunt alerted her sisters and brothers that something was wrong and soon my relatives were there, trying to kick the door in. The three locks plus the black pole called the police lock made it impossible to get in. I was scared and crying because I thought someone was trying to break in and kill us, so I climbed under the bed next to Aunt Betty and tried to pull her under there with me. Soon I heard a familiar voice yelling up from the street calling me by my nickname, Peaches. They said, "Come to the window Peaches." My aunt and uncle said "Find the keys Peaches and throw them down to us." I climbed over Aunt Betty's body and got the keys off of the dresser. I went to the window and dropped them five stories down to the street and then went back to hide under the bed. They came in and found me under the bed holding Aunt Betty's arm. They frantically called an ambulance and then began raiding Aunt Betty's closet, taking out mink coats, and all of Aunt Betty's money and jewelry.

Why did they take her things?

Just being ghetto and thirsty for some money, gold and furs. But my mother had a trick for them though.

I said to them, "Put that back, that's Aunt Betty's stuff," but they put me in the kitchen and told me to sit down. By the time the paramedics took Aunt Betty's body away, my aunt and her brothers had finished packing everything up and my mother was walking in the door. I jumped up and ran to my mother and started to tell her everything. All I heard was, "Uh, uh. Ya'll ain't taking a damn thing out this house." My mother took the first punch and connected with my aunt's face from the projects, the next thing I knew my mother was dragging her by her hair while stomping her and punching her in her face. My uncles were yelling "Let her go Coffee, let her go," while they tried to pull them apart. When they parted my mother had a patch of my Aunt's hair in her hand, and my aunt had a big bald spot on her scalp. My mother kicked ass and made her point. After the funeral my mom ended up giving them a couple of pieces of jewelry that was passed down from their parents but none of what Aunt Betty had earned. Mom kept the rest for us.

What was it like after she
buried your Aunt Betty?

My mother was sort of sad that she wasn't there when Aunt Betty died, she thought that she could have made a difference if she was there. She took it kind of hard, and to me, she started to hustle even harder to make sure that her own children wanted for nothing as well. She was doing what she was doing to make a better life for us. She gave us a lavish lifestyle just like hers. We had six or seven pairs of Pro-Keds, (the Nike of our day), every color sweatsuit and dress clothes from Macys. When Christmas time came around we had every new toy that came out on the market. I loved the lavish gifts my mom gave me, but I loved her more. I just wanted to be around my mom. I hated when she was gone, but I hated when she was around because I knew there was going to be some drama. Overall, I hardly got a chance to see her.

*Tell me what it was like
growing up at home with your
mother after your Aunt died.*

There was a lot of company and a lot of new stuff all the time. My mom became even more highly regarded in her circles and was becoming so good that she didn't have to hustle all the time. She was a Ghetto Queen who had chosen the fast life. She had a loving and loyal group of friends who after every night of hustling and shopping, would retreat to their favorite after-hours spot and drink until the wee hours of the morning. We kids would hear them stumble into the apartment early in the morning, talking loud, and arguing.

What were they arguing about?

Nothing, really it was just their way of communicating and teasing each other.

Go on.

The loud talking and arguing would often turn to laughter and we would be awakened to see my mother come in with shopping bags full of presents and jewelry. She would have us try everything on and then model it in front of her friends. While they made drinks and folded their match book covers to sniff their coke out of hundred dollar bills, she checked the lengths on the pants and sleeves to see if anything had to go back to the store. Next I tried on the diamond earrings and gold necklaces and my five-year old brother tried on his new diamond rings.

Where were your eldest
brother and sister?

I don't know. They always seemed to be doing what they wanted out in the street, but she always had something for them too.

 After we were fitted with our sparkling jewels and fully clothed, we ran to different mirrors in the house to see our new stuff. By then my mom was getting her groove on with her friends and they were talking loud again. My mom would say," Okay, now what do you say?" In unison we said, "Thank you mommy." "Okay now go back to your room and put your new jewels in your jewelry boxes and hang up your new clothes." We gave her some kisses and then put our things away. I always wanted to hang around a little longer to see if I could learn something new, so she let me stay for a few minutes more. Afterwards she sent me on my way.

What did you and your little
brother do when your mom's
party was over? Who fed you

guys in the morning and
supervised you?

Supervision, huh, there wasn't any, I did the best I could in the kitchen with being only ten- years old. As morning turned to the afternoon we tiptoed around the house while my mother and her crew were fast asleep. As usual, there were bottles of Johnny Walker Red, Champagne, and piles of cocaine left scattered on the tables. I used to creep into my mom's room and run my fingers through the coke, imagining I was plowing through the streets. Once I finished playing in the snow, I licked my fingers and sniffed some up my nose like I had seen my mother doing. This time I couldn't stand the medicine taste that the coke had, so I washed it down with a drink. Afterwards, the coke taste dripped down the back of my nostrils, and down into my throat. It was nasty at first, but every time after that, it got better.

Was that your first drink ever?

Yup, Johnny Walker Red.

What about the cocaine?

Nah, I always tasted the residue of coke that was left on the playing cards, table tops and especially sniffed what was left off of those hundred dollar bills.

How old were you and your little brother then?

I was about 10 and he was 5 but I had been using cocaine well before the alcohol.

What happened next?

I had just tasted the coke and drank the last of the Johnny Walker when my mom woke up and asked, in a groggy voice, what was I doing. "Nothing," I said, "Can we go to the park?" "No," she said, "Take this money and go around to Aunt Regina's house and tell Justeen I said to feed you." "Okay," I said and started to get dressed. I asked her if I could wear my new Pro-Keds and my new sweat-suit. Still hung over, she said, "Yes. Now go!"

Who was Justeen?

She was around 17 years old and she was my favorite cousin. She was Aunt Cookie's eldest daughter. She was a prostitute who walked the streets at night, but when she was home she would keep her brothers and sisters from picking on me and calling me "the yellow banana". She was the one who always made sure I was well taken care of. She never did anything bad to me.

Go on.

I got dressed and got my little brother dressed. I was drunk as a skunk and staggered around the corner to my cousin's house. I don't know what possessed me to do a cartwheel but I ran halfway down the block with my little brother and put my hands out, only to find out that my arms would not support me. I ended up lying on the ground with my face in pain. I could feel the flesh around my eyebrow and cheekbone throbbing. My face had gotten scraped on the pavement just outside of my Aunt Regina's building.

My cousin Justeen saw me and ran out. "Are you all right?" she asked, picking me up. "Your face is bleeding and, you smell like a drunk! What have you been drinking?" "Johnny Walker Red," I told her. "What? Where is your mother?"

"She's home asleep, she said for you to feed us. Hunh, take the money." Justeen took me in the house, bandaged my face, fed me and my little brother, then made me lay down in order to sleep off that liquor.

3

Good, I am happy we are back to your Aunt Regina's house, because that's where it happened, isn't it?

Yes.

Are you ready to tell me what you remembered that made you scream like that a few minutes ago?

Uh huh. Okay, I am. But Allan it's disgusting.

It's ok. I know its going to be painful, but I want you to take your time and tell me everything they did to you.

Okay.

The vision of big hands, thrusting tissue into the small vagina of a child came to me. I saw hands probing and touching the tiny bald pubic region of a little girl in the bathtub. Hands, violent and urgent, were doing things to her in the bathroom, the bedroom, the rooftops, and the back yards. Violent filthy things that no child should have to endure.

It was my sixteen year-old cousin Belinda (Justeen's younger sister), sticking tissues in the vagina of this 7-year-old, lying face down on a bed. Then, I could see the same child awakened from her sleep in pain because of a forced entry into her bottom by Belinda's 19-year old boyfriend. On dark lonely nights at home, when her 18-year old cousin Desmond (Justeen's brother) babysat her, he forced oral sex with his pissy penis upon this small helpless child once her mother went out and left them alone.

I saw dark basements and tarred rooftops, boys and men and a little girl. I saw them lure her into bedrooms with the promise of candy or toys and then terrorized her. I heard them make her swear not to tell or else they would kill her.

Who was that little girl
Conscious?

As puddles of tears built up on my bottom eyelids and went rolling down my face I felt a knot so hard in my throat that I thought I was suffocating. Then I answered,

I screamed because that little girl was me. Allan, It was me. My nasty ass cousins did that to me. Every male friend of the family that I trusted, and looked up to betrayed me. They all tainted my innocent soul.

So the tissue and the vagina,
can you make a connection
with yourself and your
insecurities with wiping little
girls?

Yes, that's why it was painful for me to touch little girls with tissue, and why I didn't want to see them naked.

Think hard. What else does
that mean to you?

That means that every time I had to go into the bathroom with them or bathe them it reminded me of me when I was little. It reminded me of a little girl being abused but I couldn't see that that little girl was me, all this time. With frustration I have been trying to make that connection all these years and I haven't been able to do it. I thought there was something wrong with me. I thought I was a freak or something. My perpetrators had me feeling insecure all my life and thinking I was crazy. All because they abused me and used me for their sick satisfaction. Somebody probably did it to them and in turn they did it to me, but I won't continue their madness, I won't continue their sick cycle. I am breaking this mad cycle right now.

Good, that's the connection,
good! That's right break the
cycle right now, you are strong,
and you are a survivor not a
victim. Now, can you

remember other things that happened? If you can let's flush it all out Conscious, it's the only way you are going to get better.

I know, I want to get better. I have to get better.

Go ahead tell the rest.

There was about sixteen of us in Aunt Regina's two-bedroom apartment, boys and girls. The kids, ranging in age from toddler to young adults, running around. My cousin Belinda and her boyfriend would make me watch them at close range having sex. Other times she would call me into the bathroom when she was menstruating and made me watch it drip and play with it. Other times while we were in the bathroom she wet tissue and put it between my legs. And then there were times when she made her younger brother Gerald, have sex with me and do things to his bottom.

There was a friend of our family who lived on the floor above Aunt Regina. Her son's name was Lucas. He was 16 at the time and would lure me to his house with toys and cap guns. Once we were in his room, he would try to penetrate me, but his penis was too large for my small body. I would tell him to stop, but he wouldn't until he was satisfied, then he gave me the toy guns and threatened me not to tell anyone. Next there was a boy named Jimmy. He would take me to the roof of my Aunt Regina's building and it would be the same story. Only Jimmy was slick, he would tell me that if I wanted to have a shape like my sister and girl cousins, then I should let him do it to me. So, I did.

How did that make you feel?

Dirty, sticky, sneaky, and guilty like a bad girl.

You seem a little agitated do
you want to stop talking now?

No I'm okay.

*Okay then is there more
abuse?*

Yes. The worst of them all.

*Why do you say that, what
could be worst?*

Worse because of who it was.

Who was it?

My big brother.

*I thought he and your sister
weren't around.*

They weren't, it happened when he came back.

From where?

California.

What, I don't understand, when
did they go to California?

Right after Aunt Betty died my sister and eldest brother became hard to deal with. I don't know, maybe they were acting out or something. They both were really close to her because she provided them with the emotional love and affection that my mother didn't. We all loved her cooking and her parties. She was our mother when our mother wasn't around. After Aunt Betty died my mom tried to step into her shoes, but I guess my sister and brother rejected her...I am not real sure what happened, all I know is they were always threatening to go live with my brother's father in Cali. After a while I guess my mom took them up on the idea, and sent them to live in California. My youngest brother stayed home with my mother and me.

Why did they come back?

My brother got busted with a gun in school and my sister began to feel left out because of the favoritism my brother received from his dad.

So what happened when they
came back to New York?

Drama.

My mom set their rooms up again with all the things that they would need. Once I knew that they were on their way back to New York, I told everybody in the neighborhood. I was running around telling everybody that my big brother and sister are coming back to New York.

Was there trouble when they
came back?

Yeah. As time went by and my brother got reacquainted with the neighborhood. First, he found some buddy's to hang out with and eventually he started selling weed and carrying a gun. My mother had the nerve not to approve of him having guns and drugs in the house. He was just following what he saw her do, so they argued a lot. Often my brother's punishment for disobeying my mom was to baby-sit my little brother and me.

Where was your sister?

She lived at home with us for a minute but then she just ran away.

Why?

She found a boyfriend downtown named Georgie and fell in love with him, so she never made it home in time for the curfews my mother set. And when she didn't make it home in time, my mother would whip her ass with an extension cord.

There was tension and drama between my mom and my big brother and sister. She had strict rules and regulations this time and my sister was the first to test her. My mother took the position that if you didn't abide, then you had to move out, and my sister rebelled. She soon ran away from home. She didn't go too far though. She went to live with her paternal grandmother down in Harlem, not far from us. We didn't see her much after that though. She went to school down there, too. My mom got stressed out about it for a minute and tried to make her come home, but her grandmother stepped in and promised to take responsibility for her. I missed her, though, and could have used her guidance and protection.

Okay so let's get back to your brother. You said he baby-sat you when your mother went out right?

Yes.

Did anything happen like when you were left with your cousin Desmond?

Worse.

One evening, when my brother had baby-sitting duty, he and I were sitting on my mother's bed watching Hollywood Squares, laughing at Paul Lynde. My brother said, "Gosh, if I had listened to my father when he used to talk about all of these celebrities in California, I would know the answer to these questions." Among the contestants that night was Jamie Morgan. She had very noticeable breasts, which she felt compelled to touch every time she said something. My then 17-year-old brother started saying, "Don't do that." He was talking to the TV screen, "Oh stop, Don't touch them like that. That's making me hot." The next thing I knew, he was violently snatching my pants off and laying himself across me in the sign of a cross, holding me down, pushing his penis between my legs. He couldn't even face me, because he knew what he was doing was wrong. He humped up and down until he ejaculated.

He jumped up and ran to the bathroom without saying a word. He left me there, looking down, asking aloud, "What's this stuff?" I felt abandoned, shocked and confused. I wanted to know what this white stuff was that soiled the crotch of my underwear and legs.

How old were you?

Eleven or twelve.

What happened next?

For all that had been done to me before, I had never seen sperm, but always felt sticky after, not really knowing why. But, now I saw an abundance of this liquid all over my legs. I started screaming at the bathroom door and calling my brother's name. I kicked the door, but he wouldn't even acknowledge me.

What happened next?

I can't remember any more of what transpired past that point. I wonder did I take my underwear off and hide them somewhere? When did he come out of the bathroom? Did he threaten me not to tell anyone? I can't remember Allan. But, I know that I didn't tell my mother or anyone else. He killed a very sacred part of my little body in just a few minutes and left me wondering what I had done to deserve it.

Why didn't you tell your
mother?

I was scared to death of her crazy ass. I thought she might get angry and I didn't want to take that chance. Sometimes when she got angry with me she would slap me, it seemed, hard enough to take my head off my shoulders. I wore glasses, so when she slapped the shit out of me, my glasses would go flying off my face. Sometimes I would get beat with an extension cord or sometimes a coat hanger, and had my privileges taken away. She was like a steam locomotive train plowing down everything in its way when she was angry.

Soon after though, I began playing with dolls, positioning them in the way that my brother had positioned himself on me. My younger brother and one of his little friends, named Roc, took notice. They said, "Oooh, you making them do something nasty." They told my mother what I was doing. My mother's response was to take the dolls away and ask me why I was making the dolls do such nastiness. I didn't really answer. I was terrified of her and never told her.

Who did you talk to, do you
remember what type of outlet

you used to deal with all of this?

Yes, I used to talk to God and ask him why he brought me to this forsaken place, and what I was here to do on this earth. My outlets were athletics and building a strong facade. I even began to change the way I looked.

What do you mean?

I became even more muscular and boyish-looking. I even began to have dreams of being a military general covered in armor.

I had to go inside of myself to find someone strong to talk to. I used to have dreams that I would be flying over the deserts of Egypt with large dunes, and pyramids. I dreamed that I was a general, leading troops into battle. I don't know who we were fighting, but when we fought I was the leader fighting hundreds of soldiers upward on a sandy hill with a long staff as my weapon. I have had this fixation on Egypt for as long as I can remember.

I heard a voice once when I was small while I was lying in the bed, and actually had a conversation with God. One time, I remember it was God, and me kicking it. We were talking about my life, and God described my previous life as one of power and royalty. He asked me what kind of life I wanted to have this time. I said that I wanted to experience a life of difficulty this time. I wanted to suffer the way I had seen peasants in the street suffer with disease and poverty. During my conversation with God I chose this life, full of trial and grief, and His response was, "So be it."

4

*So you say you changed how
you looked?*

Yeah.

Why?

**Because I was tired of being picked on and abused.
I cleverly figured that if they were looking for a
pretty little girl to abuse, then I should change
myself into a tough-looking little boy, in order to
hopefully be overlooked. You know, sort of like
"Darwin's Theory" "Survival of the fittest." Or the
way an Army soldier camouflages himself in battle.**

*Umm that's an interesting
connection you have made
Conscious.*

Yes it is. Allan you know that we as humans have a built-in will to survive. We will change our spots or miraculously mend our crushed bones in order to survive.

Yes people do it all the time.
How soon did you go through
your transformation?

It started as soon as I saw I could not defend myself. I remember begging my mother to let me take karate classes and lift weights. I just knew that I had to defend myself against male friends of the family, my brother and my cousins. I soon became very aggressive and athletic in school. I needed to be in control of other children and became intimidating to them.

I got involved with gymnastics, karate, swimming, and basketball, because it was important to me to be superb in each area in order to strengthen myself. I began to distance myself from the female gender and began to disguise myself as a boy with the hopes of being overlooked by any male predators that were looking for a weak little girl.

So you didn't want to be a girl
anymore?

No, I hated being a girl all my life. The thought of being a female had faded away. At the age of 7 or 8 I began to consider and carry myself like a little boy. I wanted to be mistaken for a male. I studied the way males stood, walked talked, ate, laughed, ran, wore their clothing, wore their hair cuts, breathed, sat, smiled, spoke, interacted with other boys, interacted with females, yelled, danced, cried fought, and then began to mimic them.

It was important that I mastered these skills and fit in comfortably among males. I found it necessary to be accepted as a male and responded to as a male, in order to prevent any further sexual abuse.

How did the people and adults
in your neighborhood respond
to you?

I got teased and called a tomboy a lot. But after a while I started to blend in and become accepted as the neighborhood tomboy. A pretty tomboy.

I was beyond being a tomboy though. I had this insatiable need to be superior to boys. From the time that I could push a weight into the air, I did. I just had to be stronger than anybody and had this burning need to excel in anything that required strength. I did more than the required amount of sit-ups and push-ups in karate. I was almost always the only girl in any of these activities which meant I had to prove my skills against boys my age and size. That was fine with me because I was obsessed with not being a weak little girl anymore.

What other kinds of activities did you have growing up in this shell?

Ha, ha. Activities? Real activities were what the kids in the suburbs had during their summer camps out in Long Island. In Harlem we had the school of hard knocks and street sense.

We hung a milk crate on a wall to play basketball, shot tops in the street, stickball, tag, hand-ball against the tenement wall. For extra fun we ran through the backyards throwing rocks at people's windows, stray dogs, cats, and each other.

Toward the middle of the summer, Benny, the number man, would throw the best block parties. The deejays would hook their equipment up to the wires at the base of the city lamppost and rock the block with music. All of the boys on our block including me looked up to Benny because he frequently showed us that knot of money he kept in his pocket. We all wanted to be number runners and loved to be around when Mike, another runner, came to Aunt Regina's place to write her favorite numbers. We watched as he wrote them down and after he gave her the receipt we followed him out of the building begging him for a dollar. Often in the course of following him, we'd get sidetracked by guys in the hallway bending over throwing dice at the wall. There were dollar bills on the hallway floor next to their feet and six guys waiting around for their turn to throw the dice. A fight almost always ensued during these games. We loved the action.

Allan why did you ask me what kind of an outlet I chose?

> *Well because it is typical*
> *among young children who*
> *have been molested to*
> *assume other identities or act*
> *out in some compulsive*
> *manner such as killing small*
> *animals that they can*
> *dominate. Sometimes children*
> *start fires for attention and as*
> *they become older they may*
> *have the tendency to become*
> *molesters, pyromaniacs,*
> *nymphomaniacs, pedophiles,*
> *kleptomaniacs, sociopath,*
> *transsexuals, serial killers or in*
> *your case develop a sexual*
> *identity crisis.*

A sexual identity crisis, wow, is that what I have? Do you think that's what I have had since I was a kid?

Yes you have had all of the
trauma and behavior to
support this Conscious.

Yeah you have a point there, Allan.

Why do you say that?

Well if you look at the cases of the Menendez brothers, Jeffrey Dahmer, Ted Bundy, David Berkowitz, Charlie Manson, and other sexual offenders, most of them have had some sort of sexual abuse in their background. They all began acting out in their childhood and then eventually became monsters who continued a sick cycle of abuse. Their twisted minds caused them to choose the outlet of serial killing to deal with their inner filth. Their behaviors could have been avoided if only adults would stop touching the children. We create these monsters.

Allan something very bad happens in a child's mind, then death takes over their soul when you introduce sexual abuse, and incest into their innocent lives.

They start to build all kinds of defenses and sick thoughts until they become old enough to lash out and hurt someone or inflict self-pain. It s a wonder after all these years God gave me the ability to wake up and realize what I was doing before I hurt anyone or hurt myself anymore. Allan ...I wish people would stop touching little children.

> *Conscious you have been blessed.*

Yes I have Allan and you were the vessel that carried the blessing to me. Thank you.

> *Don't start thanking me so soon because we are not finished yet.*

What do you mean?

> *Well there is a special group that I want to put you and several of your peers in.*

What is it?

It's called a Marathon Group.

A Marathon Group? Ohhh no, I heard about that group.

Calm down, it's a group that I will monitor. You and 4 other people will stay awake for 24 hours telling your entire life stories, while I probe each one of you with questions in order to help you make sense of some of the things that have happened in your life. This process is called in-depth self-examination, or introspection. In addition to my questions, you will ask yourself questions, and draw your own conclusions. I am just there to help you think. In some cases you may regain memories

about things that have been
lost due to drug abuse,
physical abuse and
psychological abuse. As the
group moves on you will feel
comfortable enough to talk
about things that you have
never shared with anyone.

I don't know about that Allan.

Don't worry what ever is said in
the group stays in the group.
You are at an excellent point in
therapy to gain from this group.

Well you haven't misled me yet so when do we
start?

Wednesday, but this is what I
want you to do between now
and then.

What?

I want you to take this
notebook and keep a journal of
everything you can remember
about your past and anything
new you remember in the
week to come. Okay?

Okay.

I could see the look of concern and partial relief on Allan's face. I had stopped crying by now and was sitting up in my chair like a plant that had been nourished and fed after weeks without water. I felt relieved and revived from pouring out all of those memories.

During your free time I want
you to sit down at a table and
let the residents in the house,
one at a time confront you on
your past and the things that
you have learned about

*yourself. Maybe they can
probe you and perhaps free up
more of your repressed
memories.*

Okay.

*And finally I want you to carry
this sign wherever you go.*

What sign?

Allan walked over to his closet and pulled out a
small sign and began to write the words "Please help
me find out who I am?"

**Awe come on Allan you're not gonna make me carry
that sign around are you?**

*You said you wanted to get
well didn't you?*

Yes.

Then let me show you how.

Damn.

*You said you changed the way
you looked right?*

Yes.

*Well who are you really? I
mean, you hid behind this
image of a boy all these years.
Don't you want to know who
the real you is?*

Yeah, I suppose so.

*Okay, let me ask you this, are
you happy with what you see
in the mirror?*

No.

Why not?

Because, I often see a male image that I have never really felt comfortable with deep down inside.

> *Then I ask you, now that you*
> *used the male image as a*
> *defense and you no longer*
> *need that defense, will you*
> *now help that beautiful little girl*
> *come back out?*

Tears began to puddle on my eyelids again because I knew it was time to now let go of the boy that protected me for so many years. Now I was scared.

Allan that's gonna be hard.

> *Yes I know but you have just*
> *tackled the biggest part,*
> *regaining your memory. It will*
> *be okay. I will help you*
> *through your transformation if*
> *you want to change back. You*
> *all right with that?*

Yeah but will that mean I will have to start wearing dresses and stuff.

We could try to see if you like it.

I already know I don't like it.

Have you ever worn a dress?

Yes when I was little.

Well if you like, I will have one of the female counselors work with you. I am going to tell you now, that it's going to be hard, and if you don't like it at least you tried.

Okay I'll give it a try.

Pick up your sign. Let's go downstairs and set up a small desk and two chairs for you in the dining room before the afternoon seminar on AIDS begins. We have a great guest speaker visiting our facility, so her presentation will be an informative one. Let's go.

Sister, why are you sitting at this table with that sign?

Because Allan told me to.

Why what happened to you?

I had repressed memory.

Repressed what?

Repressed memory.

What the hell is that?

That's when you forget a part of your past because of a traumatic event.

What you mean by that? Break that down for me Sis.

All right, check this out right. You know how a person who has been in a car accident goes into a coma because his injuries are so traumatic.

Yeah.

Ok, do you know why they lose consciousness?

No, why?

Because there is so much pain and damage that the body needs to shut down in order to protect and repair itself.

Alright, then what?

Okay you know how the doctors tell the family of the victim to talk to that person while he or she is in a coma and touch the bottoms of their feet in order to stimulate them?

Yeah, so they can help wake them up right?

Right.

So what does that have to do with you?

Well similarly a part of my mind was in a coma. You know sort of unconscious due to a traumatic event.

What traumatic event was that?

I was sexually molested when I was little and the pain was so traumatic that my mind shut down a part of my memory for protection and repair.

Oh, okay I'm with you. So how did you get your memory back?

By coming into this drug program and receiving the stimulus from groups and sessions with Allan.

Oh, so Allan helped you regain your memory?

Yeah.

How?

He just kept stimulating my mind by asking me a lot of questions about my past and my deepest secrets during groups.

That's deep. Then what happened?

Then that part of my mind that was in a coma so to speak, woke up and I am now Conscious of my entire childhood.

Word. Yo, that's deep sister. So how do you feel now?

Oh, I'm shocked about all of the bad things that I remember, but I feel like a ton of bricks have been lifted off my shoulders.

Is there more stuff that you remember?

Yeah a little more, I am writing it down in this journal right here.

Well what's up with that sign, who are you?

I don't know yet. I am trying to figure out who the real me is.

Unh, you are starting to make me think about my past as a little boy, and some of the things that happened to me sexually. Maybe if I take a closer look at myself I may uncover something that will help me make sense of my life and I how I ended up here too. Well, I am happy for you Sis, keep working on yourself and God bless you.

Alright you too, my brother.

Conscious the seminar is about to begin, bring your stuff into the auditorium so we can hear what the guest speaker has to say.

Okay let me finish writing this paragraph.

This whole thing is crazy. I can't believe I remembered all that stuff about my past. I guess God waited until I was off the street and into a controlled environment to reveal my past. I guess if God would have allowed me to recall my past while I was out there in the street pimping girls and smoking crack, then I might have bugged out and never made it to this program. I would probably be dead or would have started using even more drugs if I would have gotten my memory while I was out there. Thank you, God and thank you for Allan. He is the best friend I have ever had. I love him.

Come on Conscious it's starting.

Ok I'm coming.

Seminar was informative. I sat down with the rest of the other 175 residents and counselors in the auditorium and listened to our guest speaker. She started off by telling us that AIDS was the number one cause of death among African

Americans, but there were new drugs on the market that were helping people with AIDS to live longer. She strongly urged all of us to get tested because not knowing your status could kill you. She then listed the ways you can contract the virus. The list included infected needles, coming in contact with infected body fluid, blood transfusions, and unprotected sex. She then went on to tell us the ways you couldn't catch the virus: that list included drinking after someone infected, kissing, or hugging someone infected.

Afterwards, she spoke to us about how HIV Positive infants born to mothers infected have a chance of developing their own blood system and becoming normal. She also said that the chances of a child being born HIV positive are greater, if the mother is not taking any medication, and substantially less if the mother is taking medication before and during her pregnancy. She said that each year three million kids contract a sexually transmitted disease and 25% of new HIV infections occur in people under the age of 22.

Her closing statement revealed that the transition from HIV positive to AIDS is determined by a person's immune system. In some cases, a person can make the transition soon after contracting the virus, or in other cases a person can stay

HIV positive for a decade or more without developing AIDS. It varies from person to person.

When the seminar ended there was a question-and-answer forum in which the residents got a chance to discuss their concerns. I didn't ask any questions because I knew I didn't have unprotected sex with anyone nor did I have a blood transfusion, and I never shot dope and never came in contact with anyone whose body fluids were infected. I knew who all of my partners were so I wasn't worried about being HIV-positive. Anyway, I was up to my seventh month in treatment and I wasn't required to take the test until my 11th month. First, I have to sort out this repressed memory stuff then I'll take the test. I told myself I still have time.

How was the seminar?

It was good.

Have you ever been tested?

Yeah when I had Pneumonia a couple of years ago. It was negative.

Were you getting high around
that time?

I been getting high all my life Allan, but I got into the crack game shortly after that and I started selling drugs out of a crack house with my cousin.

During that time how many
partners did you have?

One, my cousin.

Your cousin? Which one?

Justeen, the one that used to care for me as a child. She was the only one who saved me from being molested when she wasn't out prostituting.

Was your cousin tested?

Yeah, she said she got tested after her last John.

Was it negative or positive?

She said it was negative.

> *How soon after her last john*
> *did you start having sex with*
> *her?*

I am not sure?

> *Then how do you know that*
> *she didn't have the virus while*
> *she was with you?*

I shrugged my shoulders.

> *How many partners did you*
> *have after you were tested?*

None, I met up with my cousin a week after I was
tested and came home from the hospital for
pneumonia.

> *Conscious you know that*
> *when we are out there getting*

high we do all kinds of sexual
favors to get drugs.

Yeah, I know but I am sure that if she was infected then she wouldn't have been with me. Besides, she told me she wasn't prostituting anymore.

You sound like you are in
denial Conscious. You heard
the information in seminar just
now. Your cousin may have
been tested but how many
partners did she have after the
test and you? You know you
can't be sure Conscious, I
want you to get tested anyway.

All right Allan calm down, I still have time. I'll be okay.

Your cousin huh?

Uh huh.

You still have a lot of secrets,
don't you?

Yeah you can say that.

How did you hook up with your
cousin?

Well I hadn't seen her in many years but I always
looked for her on the hoe stroll down by 42nd
Street, near the Port Authority bus terminal. Then
one day my sister told me that Justeen was running
a crack house Uptown on St Nicholas Avenue in the
neighborhood we grew up in, so I went to visit her.
She was so surprised to see me after so many years
that the first thing she said was, "Damn you got big
and fine. You must be about six-one. Damn you tall,
come here gimme a kiss." I said, "Damn cuz you
look like a lil sumpin' sumpin' too Ma'." And blessed
her with a big hug and a kiss on the cheek. As we
sat and talked, the bell kept ringing and customers
kept knocking on the door to buy "product". When
she answered the door she yelled, "How many, got
plenny?" The customers answered, "Gimme four

red tops, yo." Justeen said, "I only got yellow tops right now." The customer's reply was, "Okay gimme dat."

There was heavy drug traffic and she was making crazy money so I sat back, cracked open my forty-ounce of beer and started sniffing my coke. When it slowed down she joined me and took a hit too. I began to tell her that I had searched for her for years and that I loved her most out of all the cousins because she made me feel safe, as a kid. Hours seemed like minutes as we reminisced about our pasts, then she started telling me how she began prostituting and how much abuse she went through with her pimp, who was also the father of her two boys. It was so sad that we got drunk and so wide open off the coke that we began to cry together. The next thing I knew we were holding each other and kissing each other's faces. We started out consoling each other and then the next thing I knew we were laying down making love. Our attraction was crazy and passionate, but in our eyes we had each other and we would absorb each other's pain. It was a love, drug relationship that would last for three years until I left the streets and came here.

> *I want you to get tested*
> *Conscious.*

Okay Allan, don't worry, I still have time.

> *Conscious, this is the kind of*
> *stuff I want you to talk about*
> *during the marathon group*
> *next week.*

Okay.

> *Come on I want you to turn in*
> *for the night.*

Good night Allan.

> *Good night Conscious.*

Getting Unstuck

6

It was Wednesday afternoon. There were four of us plus Allan listening intently as each person told his or her story. There were boxes of Kleenex and balled-up tissues filled with tears on the floor next to each one of them. They were wet from crying about all of the tragedies and hard luck they each suffered. They spoke about all of the jobs they held, and the materialistic things they owned before they started smoking crack or shooting dope. They spoke of the lies and deceit they used to get drugs, the scams they used and the dick they sucked to get high. Some of them lost their children to government agencies, and some of them contracted diseases. The stories were gruesome and personal, but it was the way Allan helped us. It was up to each one of us to put our mess out on the table so that Allan could clean it up and give us a plan to recovery.

Allan set up one of our big roomy lounges with pillows, comfortable couches and chairs with cushions. The lounge had tall windows, wall-to-wall carpeting and a small bathroom off to the side. The tables were filled with bowls of fruit, a coffee machine, sodas and sandwich platters. There was a picture of the founder of Daytop, Monsignor O'Brien on one wall, and a telephone on a small table next to a lamp.

Everyone sat there with snot still running out of their noses and their eyes puffy from purging all of those crazy street memories out of their system. We were in our 18th hour and it was my turn to spit my story.

Conscious are you ready?

Yes.

> *Why don't you bring the group*
> *up to speed with what has*
> *happened to you in the last*
> *week. And then I want you to*
> *take off from where your Aunt*
> *Betty passed away.*

They all sat up attentively on their pillows and cushions scattered on the floor.

> *Conscious I also want you to*
> *talk about how it was for you*

growing up being sexually
confused, and the influence
your mother had on your life.
Most of all let us know how you
went from designing electrical
engineering blue prints at a
major New York utility to
selling women on the street,
and smoking crack cocaine.
Then tell us what drove you off
the streets and why you chose
to call Daytop for help.

Well to tell you the truth, it was a call that I first received which inspired me to get help for my addiction.

A call? What do you mean?
Who called you?

I received a calling from God. I mean, you might think I'm bugged out or something like that, but I heard a voice from God while I was laying in the bed

with my cousin after a week of running from coke dealers.

No we don't think you're
bugged out, what did God say?

He warned me to leave the crack house that I was living in at that very moment or else I would be dead, and while I lay there he revealed two very important things about my future.

What were they?

God said that he had a job for me to do.

And what was that job?

He said he would use me to spread a message to a large mass of people, but I am not sure what that message is yet.

What was the second thing?

He said that a disease would strike me but that it would not affect me until his work was done.

What kind of disease do you think that you will be afflicted with?

I haven't got a clue, but what I do know is that I got up out of that crack house and followed his word here. You see I know that I was chosen to do something for God because I am starting to see signs of memory recovery and that is an act of God. He is slowly developing me for something, but I don't know what yet, so I will just let him guide me with no questions asked.

Good Conscious, the topic of repressed memory is a perfect place for you to start. Bring the group up to speed with how you regained your memory.

All right, this is how it all went down.

I began to tell them all about how Allan helped me regain my memory of incest and molestation. Next I spoke about the insecurities I had with my sexuality and all about my mother. By the time I brought them up to speed I was talking about how my mom moved us to Philadelphia after Aunt Betty died.

My mother said she hit the number big, twice. And then announced that she now had more than enough money to move out of Aunt Betty's apartment and rent a duplex townhouse in Philadelphia. My mother always had something up her sleeve. I mean who hits the number twice in the same week? "Fighting Coffee Brown" was always making moves.

Did all of you move to Philly?

No, my eldest brother joined my sister and moved in with their grandmother in Harlem. So, it was only my mom, my little brother and myself in our duplex apartment in Philly.

So what was the new place like?

Off the hook.

My younger brother and I shared a room with a sliding glass door leading to a backyard. Our brand new dressers and desks acted as a partition in our bedroom, marking his space and mine. The kitchen was modern. It had a dishwasher and garbage disposal and a microwave. The stairs up to my mother's room and her bedroom were covered with wall-to-wall white carpeting. The walls were covered with long custom-made mirrors and wallpaper that matched the also custom-made shower curtains and drapes.

Over in the corner where the mirrors met sat a circular, heavy clear glass table supported by a bamboo base. That's the table they used to cut the dope and cocaine and weighed it. When she swung open her custom-made drapes, there was a well-furnished balcony that overlooked our backyard. We had a huge basement with a washing machine, a dryer, and the central air conditioning and heating system. We had gone from our ghetto fabulous apartment in Washington Heights to a middle-class neighborhood just blocks away from the world-famous Philadelphia Art Museum, where they filmed the movie "Rocky."

Why Philly?

Well because we had cousins there and besides that my mom wanted to slow her pace, provide a better environment for us and try working legitimately. So she said.

So how did your mom get a job?

My aunt helped her get a job.

How did it all begin for you guys in Philly?

When we first got to town my Aunt DeeDee helped my mother get a job as a secretary. My aunt was a smart classy lady with a lot of connections in the entertainment industry. She and her husband owned a health food store on Wanamaker Street in South Philly and she was a makeup artist and personal assistant to a famous R&B singing artist. It was a sweet beginning for what looked to be a healthier and happier life.

Why did you say that? I thought your mom was on that legitimate kick?

Well she was for a minute. I mean she worked her 9 to 5 faithfully, but the money wasn't what she was used to and her craving for the fast lane was not being satisfied. So after a while we started receiving visitors.

Visitors like who?

Old friends from New York.

My mother began inviting her old hustling buddies from New York to come stay at our place in Philly. They would stay up late, just like before and soon she began missing work. She also began hustling again. Philly was a new arena and a slower-paced town. So, she and her crew cleaned up. They were more successful than ever. They came home with big sums of money, jewelry, traveler's checks, illegally rented cars, clothes, fur coats, Chanel, and Gucci stuff just like before.

So who were the friends.

Her main two partners were Mitsy and Pinky.

My mom had this friend named Mitsy, a heroin addict. Mitsy would come back to our house after making money and pay me to squeeze the abscesses that developed on her arms swollen from daily injections of dope. All the while I'd be doing this, she would say, "Conscious don't ever let me catch you shooting no dope in your arms. Do you see what this shit does to you? Just look at my arms. You don't ever want your arms to be swollen like this, and your hands to look like mittens. You hear me!" I'd say, "Yeah, okay be still Mitsy and turn your arm over so I can get that one too." I got paid crazy money just for making a place in her arms to shoot more dope and running errands.

The cash was flowing. We were eating lobster with butter sauce for breakfast and our necks, wrists and fingers were draped in gold and diamonds; my mother's birthstone.

Who was Pinky?

The lady with the dope connections.

Pinky let me drive her brand new Cadillac Seville when she came in from New York. I'd ride my friends Diego, Prince and Bronx around in it. They were a couple of guys on the block that my brother and me got tight with. We all called her Aunt Pinky and she loved them like she loved us. Aunt Pinky made sure that we all had brand new clothes and sneakers for the summer. She was the dope lady so when she came to our house, she came to cut and bag heroin and cocaine on that round glass table in my mom's room. Her favorite utensils were a strainer, a couple of different-sized spoons to measure the dope, a razor blade, cellophane bags, rubber bands, aluminum foil and a triple beam scale.

There were so many piles of different drugs and residue in the air that if you had to go to my mother's room for any reason while they were cutting and bagging, you had to wear a surgical mask. When they completed the bagging, I watched as they counted and put a rubber band around each bundle.

> *What else was going on in*
> *your new place?*

Drama.

There was money and partying going on at our house all the time, so my friends had a ball. I even began drinking openly in front of my mom. I got into the habit too of playing the peacemaker when fights erupted. For instance, when my mother felt one of her runners weren't moving fast enough to go pick up a package, she would go off. Whenever she would get into an altercation I'd be the one to stop her from hurting someone. Or if she was trying to make a point and they didn't acknowledge her quickly enough, she would slap the shit out of them or throw a drink in their face. I was her pit bull, her bodyguard. I had her back from the time I was a kid, in part because of my size. It was a dangerous job, though. She once stabbed me in my hand by mistake while I was breaking up one of those crazy fights.

My mom started traveling back and forth between New York and Philly, making power moves. During one of those trips she met this guy named Carlo. Carlo moved in with us during his first visit to our apartment. When I first laid eyes on Carlo, I wished he were my dad. He certainly was tall and light-skinned, like me. Carlo was this half-Black, half-Italian guy. He looked Italian, but when he spoke with that doped-up, raspy-ass voice, I knew he was a Black dope fiend, straight out of Harlem. The biggest problem they had was their insatiable appetite for cocaine. Carlo loved to shoot coke and heroin, which is an especially dangerous concoction also known as a speedball, and Mom preferred to sniff her "blow."

Where was your dad at this time? Did she ever talk to you about him?

No but I kept asking.

From time to time, I'd ask my mother to tell me more about my father and his side of my family. But the questions fell on deaf ears. She would ignore me and get very quiet. The more I saw Carlo, the more I wanted to know more about my dad and that side of my family. It was funny because right around the time Carlo started living with us, I felt something deep inside me wanting to pressure my mother with more and more questions about my dad. One time when she returned home from New York, she walked in my room and handed me a newspaper article with a picture of a very handsome cop in his uniform. The article said, "Off duty transit police officer murdered during a robbery in a Harlem club." The story said the officer was sitting in a nightclub when two armed men attempted to rob the place. He was in plain clothes, but strapped with a gun. As he reached for his badge and weapon, he declared that he was an officer. As the perp swung around, the officer fired and hit one of the robbers. But, the officer wasn't fast enough to stop the other perp from firing his gun in response. The officer took one bullet to the heart and died. That officer was my father and now I had no chance to know him.

How did you react to his death?

I sat down on the steps leading to the backyard in shock. I didn't know whether to cry or to lash out at my mother for not allowing me a chance to know him. As I read further, though, I was hit with a rejection that shook me even more.

What did the article go on to say?

The article gave the burial arrangements and mentioned that only a wife and a son survived my father. I was never mentioned and it made me feel as if I never existed to him. My mother neither encouraged nor discouraged me from going to the funeral. She let me make my own decision and I chose not to go. My mother said she was hesitant to tell me about his death because after she read the article she wanted to spare me the pain of rejection and absence in my father's obituary. My questioning about my father stopped that day.

Getting Unstuck

1

Why do you look like a man?

Why do you think I look like a man? Anyway I don't want to talk about that.

> *Don't get defensive Conscious.*
> *I am entitled to address you*
> *with questions and statements*
> *relevant to your situation and I*
> *think it's a good question.*

Yeah, but why did you have to say it like that?

> *Like what?*

I don't know.

> *Does it bother you when*
> *people stare at you or ask you*
> *that question?*

Yeah.

Why?

Because I got teased about looking like a boy all my life. I guess I am kind of sensitive about it.

Did they tease you even when you moved to Philly?

Yeah even in Philly.

What was it like at school and in the new neighborhood? Did people accept the way you looked? Did you settle in quickly?

No it was a little hard at first.

Why, what happened?

At school I felt uncomfortable.

My mother put us in this catholic school called Saint Francis Xavier where we were required to wear uniform dresses. No pants for the girls, even on cold days. I didn't want to wear those old green plaid skirts with that ugly yellow blouse, knee socks and saddle shoes because when I looked in the mirror each morning, what I saw was a boy in a dress. I was really tall for my age and big-boned with close-cropped curly hair. In my eyes, wearing a dress made me feel like a weak little girl. That went against my strategy for survival. I felt a sense of achievement whenever I was mistaken for a boy, and in the clothes that I typically wore, that was often. I was used to wearing trendy boy's sportswear and I wanted to keep it that way but the nuns at Saint Francis weren't having it.

*Did your mother ever buy
dresses for you as a little girl?*

Yeah but it didn't matter though. For years my mother had been trying without success to get me to wear dresses and pretty girl clothes. After a while, she gave in and stopped wasting her money on that fem stuff.

So what about the neighborhood?

I hung out with the boys just like before. I found a group of boys to hang with on my block. We were all basically the same height and had the same strength and speed. There was Nelson, Prince, Eduardo, Vinny, Larry and my little brother. But of them all, I was the most handsome. When we walked down the street, the girls on the city bus would scream out the window for us. We would laugh because they mistook me as one of the guys. My crew was tolerant of my boyish looks and defended me against people who would tease me. Every once in a while, I'd be called a tomboy or butch, particularly when I was beating the fellas really badly in basketball. I would chase the name-caller out of the park and around the parked cars until I caught them. Once I caught them, we would wrestle and fight to the ground. In the end, we would end up laughing. And always, my crew would protect me from anyone outside of our circle who thought they could get away with picking on me. Bronx especially, would run up on a guy calling me names and say, "Yo punk. She's with us and we'll fuck you up." I was the neighborhood tomboy, one of the boys, and I didn't care about being a tomboy until people singled me out by calling me names.

As you got a little older, didn't you want a boyfriend?

Not really, although I did notice a change in my body and boys outside of our clique started having interest in me. It was a year later when I was in the ninth grade. We had all grown big enough to play on the full courts with the older guys. Now, in high school, my athletic skills were increasing and so were my breasts.

My mom bought me a couple of bras and showed me how to put them on. I was bugging. Me, Conscious, wearing a bra? I began to feel different around the guys because I could not hide my ever-so-present voluptuous shape that was beginning to form. I started to wear bigger shirts, so that they wouldn't notice my bust as I ran. I wasn't the only one of my buddies who was changing. Bronx's voice got real deep. He, the other guys, even my brother, got girls and added kissing to their activities. Was I supposed to find a girl to kiss too? I wasn't sure and began to feel insecure and left out. There were times when everybody disappeared into corners and stairways of buildings to be with their girls. Worst of all, Larry beat me in a sprint from one end of the block to the other. This was unheard of. And then, one day he took his shirt off and had muscles everywhere. His chest was growing muscles, while mine was growing flab.

> *So while they were getting girls*
> *did you finally get with the*
> *program and get a guy?*

Sort of. I finally found a guy who liked me and didn't care that I was trying to look like a boy. His name was Kendell and he could play basketball better than me. He was a little older than the rest of my friends and was well-liked in the neighborhood because of his good looks and charm. My mother became fond of him and trusted him to cop drugs for her and her friends when they were low. She accepted his presence around our house and, as time went on, he and I got close. Like me, he was tall, but brown-skinned and muscular. In the summer, while my mother was in New York, he'd pick me up from my house and we would ride our bikes around. Kendell was the kind of guy who would dare to ask me questions and say things to me that no one else would.

Things like what?

The same question you just asked me. Kendell would say, "Why do you carry yourself like a boy?"

"Mind your business." I'd say, "Don't worry about how I look." But, he kept asking me that and all kinds of other nosy questions like, "How does your mom get all that money, and why ain't she ever around?" I'd always have a smart answer. Sometimes I said things that I knew would make him playfully chase me around, grab me, put me in a headlock and wrestle down to the grass. When we were done, Kendell would say, "It don't matter how much you try to hide it, you're still a beautiful girl," and he'd steal a kiss on my lips. I punched him and chased him for doing that.

Did you like him? Were you
starting to give in?

Honestly, I was fighting the feeling he was creating inside of me but I didn't know why I still needed to be hard. I was confused. Kendell had me all shook up inside and I was trying not to show it.

So did you and Kendell start
spending more time together
and less time with the other
guys?

Yeah once in a while until things got hot.

One day when Kendell and I returned from the bicycle paths in Fairmount Park, we found my little brother and the guys hanging out on the block. Kendell and I pretended to be just buddies while we were in the presence of our crew, but my nosy little brother was catching on to us. He saw us getting closer, spending more time with each other than the crew.

It was getting dark, so we all retreated to my backyard. There we laughed and snapped on each other and slap-boxed. As 3 a.m. approached, Nelson, Prince, Bronx and Vinny headed for the backyard gate, saying good night. As they left the backyard they yelled over the gate. "You gotta leave too Kendell." Kendell yelled back, "Mind your business before I break you in half with one hand." We all laughed. Kendell and I sat out back talking for a little while longer. After a while my little brother went into the house.

Kendell was inching closer and closer to me. And I kept inching away from him. The next thing I knew we were play-fighting and he was putting me into a headlock and I was grabbing him around his waist. I was feeling more feminine than usual. So, when Kendell began to kiss me I was receptive. We were up against the wall when my body began to tingle as he pressed against me. We kissed and wrestled, and kissed and wrestled. We could see my little brother inside the house. He was beginning to doze off.

Kendell said to me, "I know you like me." Well, I was trying not to, but I was feeling this thing inside me. That butterfly feeling you get when you are sixteen years-old and someone is getting to you. "I'm going inside," I said. "I'm going in too," he said.

"Kendell, you are going to get me into trouble," I said and went in the house. He followed. We sat on my bed and I turned the television on. When I sat back down, I was amused to see that Kendell had his socks stuffed in his sneakers and his tee shirt off. I laughed and said, "Where are your clothes, Kendell?" He just smiled and reached over to change the channel. I got up and got my things ready for a shower. And afterward, he did the same. As I lay in my bed with my tee shirt and shorts on, chills ran through my body and butterflies played tag in my stomach. When he came out of the shower, he sat down on the side of my bed and as we watched a late-night show, he began to kiss my neck and my ears. I was scared to death but I knew him and I was comfortable with him. Slowly as he kissed me, he laid me on my back. Before he lay on top of me, he gently removed my shorts and his too.   I laid still and stiff as a board at first but began to respond to his guiding words. He slowly put his swollen flesh inside me. The pain was tremendous at first and I wanted to stop, but he talked me through it. We created a rhythm as one and as he climaxed, he withdrew. He told me to go take a bath again and squat down so I didn't get pregnant. After I came back to the room, I laid down. He put his arm around my shoulder and laid my head on his chest. Moments later I was sound asleep. This was my first experience with consensual sex. I did this because I wanted to.

So did you like sex with him?

Yeah, but I don't think it was the sex. I think it was the fact that Kendell stood up to me and cared about me. I had never had an experience with a guy that was so nice. We were slow and sensuous with each other.

So did your relationship grow?

No, not really. After that night my future with boys got sidetracked.

What happened?

We fell asleep lying in my bed, leaving the TV on. My little brother was sound asleep as well, on his side of the room and my mother and Carlo were out of town for two days now. It was about 8 a.m. when the door of our bedroom swung open. I woke up to see a figure, swinging and punching. I jumped up to defend myself, only to see that it was my mother "going off" on us. Kendell woke up and fell onto the floor trying to block the flurry of punches my mother was throwing toward his head. She screamed with every hit she landed on us. Carlo came running in and grabbed her, screaming, "Leave those kids alone. What do you think they would be doing while you weren't here?" Kendell was trying to grab his clothes and get out the room but she had us both hemmed up in the corner.

Did you give it to him?" my mother yelled at me. "Did you do it?" I said, "Yes, yes we did it!" and she lunged for Kendell, trying to hit him again. Kendell ducked and dodged her punches then scurried through the sliding glass door and over the backyard fence, throwing his clothes over first. My little brother sat there in his bed amused and snickering. My mom snatched my television cord out the wall and rolled my TV stand out the door saying, "No more TV for you until you can explain why you had company in the house while I was gone." All the while she was arguing with Carlo about whether she handled the situation right or wrong.

The morning after, my mother grilled me with questions about how many times we had done it and whether we used protection. Then she forbade me to see Kendell. He wasn't allowed in the house or the backyard. She said that we had been having unprotected sex in her house and she didn't want me getting pregnant by him. My mother said that we were disrespecting her house and that we should take a break from seeing each other. I liked him but I wasn't crazy about defying my mother. I remember the last time I defied my mother. I ended up with first and second-degree burns from a hot cup of

coffee. I wasn't going out like that this time, so I
stayed away from him.

Hot Coffee?

Yeah she was famous for throwing hot coffee on
someone during a fight. That's how she got her
nickname. She even proved her name once more
with me.

What did she do?

One morning she got out of bed before us. Me and
my brother woke up to the smell of coffee brewing
in the kitchen. I went to the bathroom, brushed my
teeth and then tried to wake my little brother up. He
was not budging. So, I raised my voice. He still
wasn't up when my mother stepped to our bedroom
door with a cup of hot coffee in her hand. Now, in
my mind I thought she was about to scream on him
for not getting up, when I told him to. But to my
surprise, she looked at me and asked, "Why is your
little brother sleeping on a bed with no sheets?" I

said, "He can start putting his own clothes away and making up his own bed by now, he's grown." Well, the next thing I knew she had heaved that hot cup of coffee towards my body. I tried to move away from the airborne scalding liquid, but my shoulder and my bare arm got drenched. I was getting dressed at the time so my shirt was only halfway on. I jumped up and down and called for Carlo to help. She said, "Don't bother screaming for Carlo he's not here." He must have left during the night, that's why she was in that stink ass mood. I guess that was her excuse for burning me.

I ran through the backyard, down the block and into my Aunt DeeDee, she was walking her dog. She took me in her house around the corner and put cold water and vitamin E on my arm that began to blister into first and second-degree burns. I went to school from Aunt DeeDee's house and totally withdrew from everyone. I was in my own head thinking how could my mother have turned on me like that? I was the one who always had her back. How was it so easy for her to do this? My relationship with my mother began to die from this point on. If she could throw hot coffee on me for that then what would she do to me if she found out I was having sex with Kendell again? I wasn't going out like that this time, so I stayed away from him.

So did you ever see him
around the neighborhood
again?

Yeah but we didn't have sex anymore and he became a pain in the ass.

What was it like when you did
see him?

From time to time I would cross Kendell's path on my way from playing basketball in North Philly. I met a group of girls that could play ball and Kendell became very jealous of my new relationships with them, so much so that he started calling me a dyke, and a butch. One evening when I was bouncing my basketball on my way home from the park, he stepped in front of me and blocked my path. I said, "Move Kendell." And he said, "When you gonna give me some more of that good loving, or are you saving it for those dyke bitches you been playing ball with?" "Fuck you." I said, as I pushed my way past him. He yelled, "Dyke dyke dyke dyke," all the way down the street as I walked away. Before long, he was spreading the rumor that I was a lesbian. Who knew he had a crystal ball?

Girls with girls and their girls with other girls and those girls looking like boys. Damn there were so many dykes on the public high school basketball team I transferred to. And they knew the dykes on the other high school teams that we played against, and they knew all the dykes on all the summer league teams. Damn, it was like a big closet full of dykes in basketball. And what topped it off was our coach was the biggest dyke of them all. Baby dykes being led by one big mama dyke.

By the time I reached the 10th grade the world of women's basketball had exploded onto the scene. Finally, we were in a decade where being a girl and being an athlete was acceptable and valued, so I said, fuck it let me try and get a basketball scholarship and go to college. I transferred to Ben Franklin High School because they had the best track record for getting their athletes a college scholarship. That's where I met Coach Lehigh, Crystal and the girls on the basketball team

*So what was up with your
coach? Was she teaching the
girls how to be gay or
something?*

Nah, she was harmless, she was just being her
butch self. I peeped her whole style and became
very curious about all of them.

Coach Lehigh was a short blonde white woman
shaped like a snowman. The kids at school called
her Lee. She taught physical education and
coached our girl's basketball team. Her leadership
abilities on the court were awesome, but some
students and faculty questioned her motives off the
court, especially when it came to allowing her
students to spend weekends at her house.

*Why, what kind of things were
going on at your coach's
house?*

Not what everyone thought, but I did experience something new. Coach said that she was trying to give us a chance to hang out in the suburbs and to create a bond among ourselves, but there were rumors that she was gay and she did have that certain appearance. She wore her blonde hair cropped short like Luke Skywalker from Star Wars and wore casual men's clothing. I couldn't wait to be alone with her so I could ask her a question about, not her, but me.

One morning I spotted coach in the cafeteria having her usual breakfast of Pepsi Cola with a thick slice of chocolate cake, so I put it on her. I said "Coach, how do you know if you are gay?" She asked me, "Why, do you think you are gay, Conscious?" I said, "I don't know." "Well, why would you ask me a question like that?" she said. "Well, a couple of girls on the team have girlfriends and I wanted to know what makes them want to do that." "I don't know why they do that. Why, are you attracted to girls?" "No." I said. "Not really. But, I am curious and I want to know what they do. Do you think that I'm gay coach?" "I don't know Conscious." She said, while I sat fidgeting in my seat. "What do you think gay women look like?" She asked. "They look like a guy, just like you and me." She let out a hearty laugh and began to blush. "Well look at the way you dress, Conscious. You dress in guy's clothes, you look like a guy and you act like a guy at school. Why do you do that?" "I don't know." I said. "Well, if that is your definition of what gay women look like, then maybe you are gay, Conscious."

I sat staring at the cafeteria door saying nothing more until Crystal came in the cafeteria and walked over to the line for breakfast. I said "Yo, Crystal Wusup." she said "Wusup coach, wusup Conscious." Whispering to coach I said, "Alright coach don't say anything about what I just asked you, okay?" She said, "Your secret is safe with me, Conscious."

So who was Crystal? What was up with her?

She was the point guard on our basketball team and my new best friend. Crystal helped me out with all that curiosity.

How?

She fulfilled my fantasy.

Crystal was this smooth-dressing and talking point guard on our basketball team. She was all of 5 feet 4, medium build with short hair shaped around her face, with a cute smile. She wore those men's suits called "Members Only." She had a certain type of charm that swept the girls off their feet and kept them flirting with her on the down low. You see, Crystal had a way of flirting with the girls that were supposedly straight. A lot of the guys who went to our games never realized that their girls were not only theirs, but Crystal's girls too. She was the Don Juan of the girl's basketball team at our school. There was a lot of hiding and living a double lifestyle for those girls. They got a rush from sneaking around and courting girls on the basketball team. Crystal got a rush from the flirting with straight girls right under their boyfriend's noses and them not even realizing it. Those were the same girls that came to the double header basketball games with their boyfriends, under the guise of watching the boys play, but anxiously awaiting the girls to play.

You're kidding me.

I am dead serious that's how it went down.

Even better, though, was when Crystal made eye contact with a girl in the stands, and managed to meet her in the girls locker room after the game. The girls locker room often worked to Crystal's advantage because female outsiders could casually blend in with the team and make contact with her at halftime or after the game. I watched Crystal do it all the time. Most of the times if the girl was interested in Crystal, she would write her telephone number on the back of a piece of Doublemint gum wrapper. As the girl walked by the bench where we waited for coach to substitute us in the game, she would drop it in Crystal's lap. When that happened, Crystal knew she was good to go and she knew she had someone new to creep with.

There was the playful eye contact and the purposely-light brushes up against Crystal that a girl would commit to let her know that it was on, and that she was giving Crystal the green light. The next move was always up to Crystal. These were the moves that I watched Crystal make and these were the advances that I watched girls make toward Crystal. I envied Crystal's ability to create those types of scenarios, and I envied the way she was able to get their attention. In most cases, I was in awe of how beautiful the girls were that Crystal possessed.

Crystal was smooth and well-liked by the students and the faculty. She always had just the perfect thing to say to get a chuckle. She was endowed with athletic skill as well as personality. Perhaps that's what got her all the girls she wanted. As the Don Juan of our girl's basketball team, Crystal was just as smooth as any one of those guys in the stands. I wanted to possess the smoothness and ability to juggle girls the way she did. I wanted it so much that I would pressure Crystal into giving me a play-by-play description of every move she made while being intimate with a girl. Crystal told me some stuff about her intimate moments, but she always denied me the juicy parts. I remember her saying, "Come on now Conscious, I can't teach you all my tricks. Why don't you find out for yourself?"

So when did you finally get a chance to experience your first girl?

One weekend when I spent a night over Coach Lehigh's house.

Coach went out for dinner and a movie so Crystal set me up with a blind date. At first I was amazed by the fact that this girl showed up. It reminded me of a call-girl service that I had seen on that television show Kojack. I was a complete stranger, a blind date. Crystal had sent this girl named Yvette to meet me at Coach Lehigh's house. Yvette was about a year older than me and average looking. I remembered saying to myself, "Damn, Crystal could have sent me one of those hot-looking girls like the ones she dated for me to practice on instead of someone so average looking. Well at least she was a fem.

Anyhow, she was just there to help me learn all the moves I needed to be intimate with a girl. My first response was, "Wusup? Come in." I asked her if she wanted something to drink, and she said no, so I grabbed a can of soda as we retreated upstairs to the spare bedroom. When we reached the room, she sat on the bed and I sat on the chair. Instantly, I struck up a conversation about basketball and the next thing you know we were debating whether my high school would beat her high school in the finals. In one smooth motion, I sat next to her on the bed as we continued to talk. While I was talking to her, I was checking out her body and her smile. After a while she began to look a little better than average, and I wanted to kiss her. When I began to feel comfortable with her I began to make contact with her while we laughed. You know, the way you touch someone on his or her arm or leg when something is real funny. Anyhow, the next thing I know we were looking into each other's eyes and exchanging touches. We both knew why she was there and we both knew someone had to make the first move. As our giggling subsided I took it upon myself and leaned forward to touch her breasts. She approved and placed both my hands upon them. At that moment she placed her arms around my neck and placed a kiss on my lips. We kissed very lightly at first and I kept my eyes open. Slowly we began to kiss deeply and I found my eyes closing. I knew we were about to become intimate so I got up and dimmed the lights in the room. When I found my way back to the bed I resumed kissing her and to my satisfaction she was receptive. I was anxious to see what it was like to make love to a woman so I began to take her clothes off. I must have been moving too fast because she stopped me and told me to wait. Inquisitive in my search for knowledge I adhered to her request and followed her flow. She put my hand on her breast again and touched my face softly. It was different than being with Kendell because at first I didn't get that tingling sensation and I didn't feel nervous. I just felt real anxious. I really didn't know what to do next so I just continued to kiss and explore her body. I felt her small soft hands run down the small of my back and squeeze the arch as I lay on top of her and softly nibbled on her neck. My hands began to wander and explore every part of her body. As I touched each part I envisioned in my mind what it looked like. As my hands followed the curves of the outside of her leg, they flowed smoothly to the inside of her leg. Alas, I had reached her nest. When I reached her nest I began to wiggle my fingers and play in her hair. While doing so, I noticed that she began to wiggle and push my hand lower. Slowly, two of my fingers became one with her body and she let out a moan. As we created a slow rhythm we both began to get aroused and excited, and after a while I wanted to do more. As I placed kisses upon her lips and neck I asked her what I should do next. Surprisingly to me, she pressed my shoulders down towards her nest. Astonished by her gesture, I laughed and said, "I don't know how to do that." She told me that she wanted to guide me on how to pleasure her with oral sex. That statement instantly reminded me of the same type of guidance that Kendell had shown me. I became one with her nest until she achieved an orgasm. Afterwards, she would do the same to me. That was the first time I had ever achieved an orgasm. My body shivered for what seemed twenty like minutes. After I had calmed down, I laid her head on my chest the way that Kendell had once done for me.

That summer I kicked ass playing ball. I slapped boards on every lay-up and won three trophies. When the summer was over, I entered the 12th grade where I started getting visits from college scouts. A scout from Syracuse University told my coach that she was extremely impressed with me and spoke of offering me an athletic scholarship. Coach Lehigh prepared me for the SATs and helped me fill out applications for colleges. Things seemed to be looking good for me until my mother and Carlo started tripping.

What were they doing? Were they still hustling?

No not like before.

Things were off the hook at home with mom and Carlo. I couldn't wait to get away from them.

Why, what was so bad in your house that you wanted to get away?

My mother and Carlo were constantly fighting and my mother was getting behind with the bills. To me, they spent more time getting high than they did making money.

It got so bad that one morning she almost shot his crazy ass.

What happened?

In the wee hours of the morning before we went to school, Carlo and my mother got into a loud fight, stoned out of their minds. My little brother and I heard a loud rumble, then a big thump upstairs. I thought that Carlo had thrown my mother on the floor upstairs so I ran up there to help her. When I got up there, it was Carlo who needed the help. So after I pulled my mother off of him I went back downstairs and tried to go back to sleep.

A few minutes later they fought all the way down the stairs to the kitchen. I turned over and put my pillow over my head in order to drown out the hollering and glass breaking. All of a sudden she came stumbling into our room saying, "Conscious, give me the gun. I'm gonna kill him. Carlo, don't mess with me while I'm in my kids' room. Don't come in here."

I reached to open the lid of the vent on the floor, grabbed the handgun and loaded it. I had no choice but to hand it to her out of fear that she might get violent with me. As she sat on the edge of my bed with the nozzle of the gun pointing at my bedroom door, Carlo's silhouette slowly approached. I screamed, "Carlo she has the gun, don't come in." He kept walking closer and closer mumbling "I love you. Why are you doing this?"

Pop! Pop! Pop! My mother fired, but he was still standing. My poor little brother sat straight up in the bed, out of his sleep. I told him not to move, then I screamed again, "Carlo, move!" Finally, after the third round, he ducked into the bathroom outside our bedroom door. My little brother wasn't scared of anything. He stayed right where I told him, laughing and saying, "Mommy's gonna kill Carlo, Mommy's gonna kill Carlo."

Once things calmed down a little, my mother handed me the gun and told me to put it away. As I did so, I noticed two bullet holes in our doorframe, and one in the closet. I said to myself, "Awe man, I gotta get away from this madness."

How old was your little brother
and how was he taking it?

Oh he was about 11 years old and he drank plenty of beer and smoked weed with his buddy Vinny to mask the pain he must have been feeling. To him everything was funny.

The first indication I got that things were not flowing the way they used to was when we started to get visits from our landlord. He started showing up with people, prospective tenants, looking at our apartment. The second time he did it, I recognized the person as the lady anchor of the five o' clock news. My little brother and I knew then that the situation seriously was looking like change. Here it was the beginning of my senior year and I had a good chance of earning a basketball scholarship to go to college, a college of my choice anywhere in the country. With no forewarning, I came home after school to find my mother packing all of our stuff and calling a storage company on the phone. Then, she told us of her plans. Neither my little brother nor I were moved by the bad news. We were used to the ups and downs in our house. We were used to my mother being consistently inconsistent. My brother and me put our books down in our room and slowly began to pack up the house and put our stuff in boxes. As my mother was packing up the kitchen items, she looked up at me, standing near her. "What are you going to do?"

"I'm going to stay and finish high school. I am this close to getting a scholarship. I can't leave now," I said. I felt like a grown-up. Like I was about to be on my own and there was no room for me to be a little kid anymore. My mother was dead serious.

"Where are you going to stay?" She asked, as if hoping on hope that I would show her that I was grown and come up with a solution to this problem."

"I'll find somewhere to stay," I said, and that same day, I did. I asked my boy Jeesie to ask his mother if I could stay in the empty room next to hers until I finished school and she said yes.

My mom was okay with my decision, so the guys and I moved all of my furniture across the street to Jesse's house. Jesse and his mom lived in a three-bedroom apartment upstairs from Diego. The extra room was perfect for me. Jesse's mother spoke only Spanish, so he explained to her that I needed a place to stay until I finished school and that my mother would send her food money and money for rent. Jesse's mother said yes, but asked a few times in Spanish how a mother could leave her 17-year-old daughter behind to move to another state. My mother knew that I was a best friend to all of the Puerto Rican and Dominican guys that I hung out with, and she knew that I would be comfortable in a household where Spanish is the first language. So, in her view, I would be all right if she sent a little cash, once in a while.

A week later our house was emptied and my mother and Carlo were ready to go. While the movers were placing the boxes on the storage truck, my little brother and his friend Vinny disappeared. My little brother was upset that he and I were being separated. We looked up and down the block for them. They were nowhere to be found. While my mom and Carlo grew increasingly impatient, the guys and me covered as much ground as we could on our bikes. I thought they ran away. As the sun had begun to set, we dismounted our bikes and sat on the steps of our now-empty place waiting for them. An hour later we saw two heads bobbing up and down on bikes, a block away. We got up to meet them. And as we circled them on our bikes and asked them where they had been, they just smiled with those dry ass lips you get from smoking weed. They reeked of beer and their eyes were bloodshot from smoking weed. They had gone off to have a farewell celebration the way drinking buddies do. My mom came out of the house and said, "Vinny, your grandmother called for you two hours ago." He shrugged his shoulders. To my little brother she said, "Boy look at your eyes. You have been drinking and smoking. Get off that bike and give it to your sister. And get in the car." As my brother got off his bike he had puddles of tears in his eyes. He walked over to all of his boys and gave them all a pound. My little brother then hugged me and said, "Goodbye." As they drove off, tears rolled down my face and I screamed down the block, "Go ahead leave me, go, I don't give a damn, I'll be okay all by myself its better this way."

I wanted to go too, but I knew that I had to stay in Philly so that I would make it to college. If I followed my mother to New York who knew when I would get back in school again? I wanted to stand alone, and not need anyone, but inside I felt like I couldn't function one minute without them. I felt like a bike that had just been pushed off its kickstand.

> *So you felt lost without them huh?*

Yeah, for the first time I began to feel like I had no one to be with. There were always my cousins, my brothers or my crazy ass mother and her crew. My family-life was marked with insanity, but they made me feel complete. I missed them already.

So you got what you wanted,
then didn't want it huh?

Exactly, I was like a battered woman who wanted to go back to her abuser. You know there is a saying that we can't stay away from the things that harm us. What's up with that Allan?

I don't know I guess we
probably all have that bit of
sickness in us.

Yeah that sure is true because, when I did get the separation from my family, that I had been asking for I should have embraced it. I clearly had not recognized the benefits of liberation from my sick family. I had not realized that I got exactly what I had always asked for when my mother left me in Philadelphia because I too, was just as sick as they were. God gave me a chance to move on and develop without them but I couldn't see that then. I was so stuck on them and lonely that the first chance I got, I went to New York in search of my family.

I walked into a courtyard surrounded by dilapidated
buildings except for one, on 147th between seventh
and eighth in Harlem. People were quickly moving
in and out of the courtyard area. There was one
huddle of people surrounding this one guy over in
the corner. There were quick exchanges of money
for drugs. At the center of the huddle was my
eldest brother, handing off drugs like he was an NFL
quarterback.

"Hey, wusup?" I said. He turned and said, "I don't
want you here in the courtyard." Then he threw me
some keys and said, "Apartment 2B."

My brother's apartment looked as if it should be
condemned. It was a one-room kitchenette, messy,
tiny and funky. There were newspapers, empty
crack vials and clothes all over the floor. The walls
were painted an ugly institutional green and the
paint was cracking and peeling off the wall. Over in
the corner by the window, there was a small cot

against the wall with someone sleeping in it. As I approached the bed a pretty girl turned over to face me. I said, "Hi, I'm Conscious." "Oh hi, my name is Tracy," she said. "I heard a lot about you." I said, "Was it good or bad?" "It was good. I heard that you were real smart and that you were going to go to college on a basketball scholarship." "Damn," I said, "You know a lot about me. Did my brother tell you all of that?" "Yup." "What are you doing in such a nasty room in such a nasty building?" I asked her.

She told me that she was my brother's girlfriend and that he was dealing large amounts of drugs. "Well, if he's dealing so much, then why is he staying in such a funky-ass place?" I said. She said because he was using just as much as he was selling, and promptly changed the subject.

"Have you seen my mother or little brother?" I asked. She said yes. She said that my little brother used to sleep over there on the floor but that my mother had come to pick him up two weeks before. She said that when my little brother first arrived in New York he lived here with my eldest brother selling drugs and getting high. She said he never got enrolled in school and that he was always getting beat up by my eldest brother when he took too long to bag the weed or stuff the vials with crack. Tracy went on to say that before my mom and Carlo got busted in New Jersey for possession of stolen goods, she found out that my little brother was being dogged-out and so she sent him down south to live on a farm with his father's side of the family.

Tracy got up to use the bathroom and I looked for a place to lay my backpack and camp out on the floor for the night. When she came out, she asked me, "Are you going to stay here for the night, and then go back to Philly in the morning?"

I told her yeah and before I could get more questions in, my brother knocked on the door. I answered. He came in and sat down on the bed. "How'd you find me?" "It wasn't hard especially with your occupation." "Don't get smart with me cause I'll send your ass right back to Philly tonight." "Don't worry, I'm not staying long." "What you doing in New York?" I wasn't really feeling my brother ever since he did what he did to me as a child, so I had little to say.

"Where is my sister and my mother?" "Your sister got pregnant by Georgie but I don't know where they are staying. When you going back to school?" "Don't worry, I'm just staying the night. I just wanted to know where everyone was, and now that I've found out all I need to know, I will be leaving in the morning." He sat down and rolled a blunt and shared it with Tracy. I got up and walked out the door.

I walked around the neighborhood a bit and then ended up on Eighth Avenue at the Chinese spot. I gobbled down my food while I looked out the ugly, scratched-up plastic window in the Chinese restaurant. I walked around to see if I saw anybody I knew and the only person I ran into was my sister's best friend, Renee and her man Seddy. She said she saw my sister the other day and gave me her telephone number. I ran to the payphone immediately to call her but the phone just rang, so I put the number in my pocket. I took a slow walk over to Seventh Avenue and then over to Lenox

Avenue and then made my way through Esplanade Gardens. I didn't see anyone I knew and my sister was nowhere to be found, so I headed back to my brother's block and to watch the drug dealers and cops play "cops and robbers."

Bored with all of the chaos on the block I headed upstairs to his apartment. When I got in, my brother and Tracy were laying in the bed, asleep, so I made a little pile on the floor to sleep on. I slept very lightly cause who knew what he might try on me. Again.

Knowing that my little brother was down south, my mother was in jail, and my sister was pregnant by Georgie, I decided to head back to Philadelphia on Amtrak. First thing in the morning, Tracy got up and made me some breakfast. After I ate, she sent me on my way. I said good-bye to Tracy and she wished me good luck in college. As I headed downstairs to the court yard, I spotted my brother in the same place I found him when I arrived the day before, doing the same thing, trading money for product. I shook my head and said, "Yo, I'm out." He said, "Aight, be good."

Do you think he knew that you
remembered what he did to
you when you were little?

Probably, that's why we were so distant.

As I started walking up the hill on 145th Street to the "A" train I felt so empty and frustrated because I wasn't able to see anyone I came to see.

Once I boarded Amtrak at 34th Street, and the trains pulled out of the station, I cried and watched the trees go by in a blur. I thought about the good times, the laughter, and the craziness I had shared with my little brother and my mother. As the train pulled into Philadelphia, I realized that I would now have to make decisions for myself that would affect me for the rest of my life, and that I would have no one else to blame for the outcomes but me.

I had to decide on what college to go to, and quick. Hopefully I could go there for the summer after I graduated because Jessie's mother was tripping and she wanted some rent money. So I decided to call my coach and ask her if that scout from Syracuse University called back yet.

As I put each quarter in the phone, I prayed that she would say yes. The phone rang and she answered. "Hello coach?" "Conscious?" she said. "Yeah, it's me. Yo my mother is in jail and Jessie's mother is tripping out about rent money. Did that scout from Syracuse call you?" She said, "Yeah, she did. She called on Friday. They want you to play for the university and they are offering you a full four-year athletic scholarship, everything included." "Yes!" I said. "They are sending you the letter of intent next week. Conscious this is your opportunity. All you have to do is finish up this semester and give me a championship ring." "All right coach no problem. Consider the championship yours. Coach, in the meantime could you hook me up with some money so Jessie's mother can stop tripping?" "No problem, I'll stop by in the morning and pay the rent." "Thanks coach." "You got it kid."

ii

It was May and our basketball team just won the city championship game. Two days later I signed my letter of intent to go to Syracuse University on a full four-year basketball scholarship. I called my new coach at Syracuse and mentioned that I had no plans for the summer. She explained that there was a summer basketball camp in session on the university's campus and that there was a counselor's position available. God was looking out for me again. Coach offered me room and board, as well as a job for the summer.

My new coach met me at the Syracuse, New York, Bus Terminal. She had long, curly shoulder-length hair and a slight build with slouched shoulders. She couldn't have been more than 112 pounds soaking wet. I was not impressed. She was so small that my initial thought was that she probably couldn't teach me much about basketball. I had this thing about size, strength and athletic ability. If you looked like you were stronger than me and you had a strong spirit, you would get more respect from me than another person would. As we drove around campus, she pointed out the various buildings and told me their names. We soon approached one of the largest athletic structures I had ever laid eyes on. It looked larger than Madison Square Garden and wider than the Spectrum in Philadelphia. She said it was called the Dome. We got out of the car and she proceeded to tell me the history of the Dome and how the Orangemen played all of their home football and basketball games there. With a look of awe and anticipation, coach told me that in the near future, women would be allowed to play in the Dome. But for now, we had to practice and play in the Manley Fieldhouse located near the Skytop part of the school's campus.

We got back in the car to drive to the dormitories and as we did, I knew I had finally made it to somewhere stable, somewhere that I would spend the next four years of my life. When we reached the dormitory I noticed coaches greeting parents and kids, unpacking their luggage. There were some skilled girls playing basketball on the courts nearby. I could tell that these weren't summer camp kids because they had a tremendous amount of form to their shots. It was a form that had taken years to develop. They were veterans because every ball they shot hit all net. As I got closer to the courts to watch, coach came up behind me and urged me to play. But, I didn't need much coaxing. I picked up one of the balls on the side of the court and began to bounce it. I did some warm-up ball handling drills and stretched my legs and arms. By the time I finished stretching the game was over and the person who had next asked me to play. We started to play and the coaches and summer-camp players gathered around to watch.

I made some fancy around-the-back passes and some sharp cuts to the basket. Every time I caught a pass and shot a lay up, I slapped the backboard with two hands. Slapping the backboard required a lot of coordination and concentration. It was a way of showboating, which is what I did a lot. The game ended with applause from the crowd at the winning basket. Coach was impressed and started introducing me to the other players and coaches. The girls on the court were juniors and seniors on the Syracuse team and I had just whipped them without any effort. Now, I couldn't wait for summer to be over and the season to begin.

During summer camp I met three girls from the Bronx, New York: Fatima, Dawn and Pam. Dawn was tall and skinny, with a front tooth that stuck out like a can opener. She lived just a few blocks from Fatima. Pam was short and chubby with crooked teeth. She was the funniest of the three and had a habit of doing cartwheels on the basketball court. Fatima was short also, but light-skinned with shoulder-length hair and unique eye coloring. One eye was blue with specs of brown, the other was gray, but the color looked different depending on the color of her clothing. She was also very well-spoken. They loved basketball and hoped to try-out for the Syracuse team.

After four years in Philly, I had finally found some people with that familiar New York accent that I'd lost and longed to regain. The first question Pam asked me when we met was "Are you from down south?" I quickly said, "No," and began explaining how I ended up in Syracuse by way of Philadelphia. She sat and listened, in awe of my story. I fascinated Fatima so much that she asked where I was going to live for the rest of the summer, before school started. I said I didn't know and was open to suggestions. So, Fatima suggested her family's house.

When camp was over, my new coach was concerned about me going to New York for the rest of the summer to live with complete strangers. But, I assured her that Fatima and I weren't strangers anymore and that Fatima's mother was expecting me. She said okay and told me that she would be in touch with me before the beginning of school.

I put my bags in Fatima's car and headed for New York City, laughing and talking with Dawn, Pam and our driver, of course. We told jokes and stories from high school days and found plenty to laugh about.

Fatima's father, who passed away when she was much younger, had been an imam in the Nation of Islam. Since that time, her mother, Mrs. Johnson-Sharif, left the Nation, but raised her son, Tommy from a previous marriage and Mustafa, and Fatima, as Muslims. Both sons were musicians. Mustafa played bass and Tommy sang the blues and played piano. Mustafa and Tommy didn't get along. Mustafa was a devout Muslim and a deadly fifth-degree black belt martial arts instructor, and the latter declared himself gay when the family broke away from the Nation of Islam. Tommy felt trapped in the Muslim customs and was not allowed to express who he really was. Mustafa swore to follow in his father's footsteps and become an imam. Mustafa would tease Tommy and threaten to kill him because of his ungodly practices. His mother, of course, forbade him to touch his brother, but couldn't stop the two from bickering.

Weren't you concerned about them finding out about your sexuality?

Yeah I was because Mustafa was crazy against it. Who knew what he might do?

Did he have a clue?

No not right away.

Fatima's mother had the same coloring as she, the light eyes and skin. She had a graciousness about her. She was so nurturing, polite and down to earth. I fit in just fine and felt secure for the moment.

As the summer went on, Fatima and I confided in each other and got closer. She told me about her ex-boyfriend who got her pregnant and how her mom made her abort it. She told me about her experiments with boys and I told her about my experiences with girls. We shared some deep thoughts and tried to comfort each other with hugs and words of consolation after each story. It seemed as though she and I had been friends for many years.

As the rest of the summer went by, Fatima and I played basketball every day. Our routine was to get up, eat, and read the sports section. While we were reading her mom made us grits and salmon with biscuits. While we ate we listened to Mrs. Johnson's favorite Blues station. She loved Charlie Parker and Billie Holiday. After we finished eating, we cleaned up the kitchen and went to the park to play ball. Some days, while we practiced basketball, Mustafa went to the second floor of the house and practiced his bass or the piano. Those were nice days, civil the way a family should be.

We all got along pretty well in the house. Occasionally though, Mustafa would annoy Fatima and I by snooping around. Mustafa was notorious for pushing open our door without knocking and going through our stuff. One day, we put a weight bench against the door to block him. Little good it did because just as we were deeply engrossed in a kiss and some incredible pelvic motion, he pushed the door and it slid aside.

The bench gave us just enough time to jump up, but not enough time to keep him from being certain of what he had seen. "Mustafa, why are you always opening up our door without knocking," I asked. "It's my house, I'm allowed to go wherever I want." We asked him what he saw and he recounted it exactly. We denied it anyway, saying that we were wrestling on the bed. Mrs. Johnson came to the door to see what the confusion was and to calm us. Mustafa told her that he saw us kissing. We declared that he had no right bustling in our room. Mrs. Johnson told Mustafa to leave our room, but said nothing more. I wondered what was on her mind about her daughter and me.

Coach called at the end of the summer saying she was able to secure a single room for me in the Brewster Boland Dormitory and that I could move in at the end of August. Fatima's mom made sure we had supplies for school and that the small station wagon was tuned up and ready for us to haul our stuff up to Syracuse. Dawn joined us on the trip back, but Pam didn't because she didn't get accepted. Her family didn't have enough money to send her to such a college.

Fatima dropped me off at my door and promised to come check on me once she settled in. I couldn't wait. I started putting my clothes away and situating my room the way I wanted. The next thing I knew, two hours had gone by. The door to my room was open so I could see all of the girls on my floor watching as their fathers pulled their trunks down the hallway, and mothers carrying their book-bags. I started to feel lonely and to long for my family. I wanted to go right back to New York. I wanted to experience them helping me with my bags and unpacking my stuff. I wanted to walk arm-in-arm with my mother and sister down the dormitory corridor as they wished me good luck in my first semester of college and made me promise to do well. This was the first time I had been alone all summer without the Johnsons or my basketball buddies there to distract me. Suddenly the loneliness began to settle in.

I was lying on my stomach crying when I heard a tap on my dorm room door. It was Fatima. When she came in she asked me what was the matter and I began to cry more. She sat next to me on the bed and began to rub my back and hair. It was perfect timing because we had waited months for a time when we could be alone together without the prying eyes of others, especially her brother. She laid down next to me and we kissed and shed tears of pain together. My pain was for the separation from my family and her pain was for me. As we kissed more intensely the cries of pain became cries of passion.

*You think that you were born
gay don't you?*

No.

*Well when did you really know
you were gay?*

**First of all, I know that I wasn't born gay and I don't
believe that I was born to be with women. Some
doctors say that there is a gene linked to a person's
sex preference, and I don't knock that, nor do I
knock the people who say they were born that way.
But, I believe in my case, if I had not been molested
and abused, I might not have ever looked for a
defense such as camouflaging myself as a boy and
seeking the safety of a woman. Being gay was a
learned behavior that seemed heterosexual in my
mind because I thought of myself as a boy when I
was little.**

So when you started to get older, then what was your excuse?

As I carried this behavior into my adolescent years, society gave me a rude awakening and showed me that my behavior was more consistent with that of a lesbian. I used to hate that word because I would always hear people whispering that as I walked by. By the time I got older, I loved everything about women. I was stuck on women and I thought a woman was someone who could fulfill me, and give me comfort and security.

What was the gay and lesbian scene like?

The Gay and lesbian scene was so distorted to me because I was often so high off of cocaine and liquor. It seemed that I always needed a dollar bill full of coke and a bottle of liquor just to go to the club.

I remember when I transferred colleges and moved back to New York with Fatima, I started hanging out in a gay club in Manhattan, called "Better Days." It was one of the hottest, hippest gay spots during the 1980s. It was the favored hangout for some of the city's most flaming queens and lesbians. There is one song by Carl B. that was like the Gay National Anthem in this place. The lyrics went, *"I'm happy. I'm carefree and I'm gay. I was born this way, from an itty bitty boy, I was born this way. You may not understand it, but I'm just an ordinary person. Yeah, I was born this way."*

The crowd jumped, every time the DJ put this song on. Up and down, the energy shot to the roof because everyone in there connected with that song. I jumped up and down too, but since then I have done some in depth self-examination in the past two weeks and have come to the conclusion that being gay was a learned behavior. I wasn't necessarily supposed to be this way, I mean...gay.

Why did you leave Syracuse University?

College was a lot harder than I had expected, especially with basketball practices, weight training and road games. The coach and I didn't become the best of friends because I was rebellious and constantly late for practice. My priorities were not in the right place. I started dating Fatima a lot and feeling sorry for myself because my mom was in jail and because I had no family. I wasn't thinking, and wasn't reminding myself that I had received a full scholarship to one of the best schools in the Northeast. I didn't appreciate that I had fairly easily achieved through basketball what millions of Black children and teenagers struggle to do, but never, obtain. I never once looked around at all of the kids who had no mothers or no fathers and some how continued to push on and complete college in their parents honor. I never once stopped to think about all of the kids that have had all kinds of abusive issues, and adversities but some how finished college and went on to become successful and productive in our society. I was stuck on my misfortunes, and stuck in so much self-pity that I thought I was the only one in the world with problems. I was *so stuck*, that I let life get the best of me.

Ultimately I sabotaged myself and let my scholarship slip down the drain. All my life, I've been good at sabotaging things that have been good for me. I quit the team and moved into an apartment off campus with Fatima. Her mom paid our rent until she was diagnosed with breast cancer during our second semester in school. We decided to move back to the Bronx and transfer our credits to New York Institute of Technology so that we could be closer to Mrs. Johnson as she endured a mastectomy.

Damn what a drastic move.

Yeah but so was everything in my life. I was making my own decisions and I thought they were right.

Tell us about your new college and family.

Going to a new college meant getting to know new people. I changed my major from pre-medical to electrical engineering. Mrs. Johnson had pep talks with me that helped get my concentration together long enough to do well in calculus and electronics. As time went on, I joined the basketball team and even received a scholarship again. Off campus, I played ball in downtown Manhattan, in the Village on West 4th Street. The public courts down there were known for attracting overseas scouts.

That's where I met Queen Latifah. Well, at the time her name was Dana Owens. She loved basketball like I did. We played on the same teams and sometimes against each other. We became friends and hung out and played basketball in the same circles. At times we hung out in the Village and partied together. I remember one day while sitting on a park bench in Washington Square Park Dana sat next to me and said, "Yo Conscious, I am going to be a rapper." I said "A what?" She said, "You know, a female-rapper. I am going into the studio this week, so I won't be seeing much more of you or hanging out in the park anymore." I said, "Okay, don't forget me when you get large." She said, "You'll always be down with me Conscious." I didn't really think much of the concept because rap was brand new, and female-rappers were unheard of. The next time I saw Dana Owens, she was on television in a rap video and her stage name was "Queen Latifah."

> *So you really know the*
> *Queen?*

Yeah that's my "dog." We spent some real special times together.

> *What else happened with*
> *school?*

I started slipping into misery again. I began to use cocaine on a regular basis at campus parties and in the dorms on the weekend. I got in the fast lane with a fast crew. I hung out with what I thought were the hip-looking, drug-using athletes. I began using cocaine so much that I would play in games without any sleep and show up at practice hung over from the night before. Because of my drug usage my basketball skills never quite met their fullest potential. For the next year or so, I drifted away from the Johnson family and got closer to the cocaine family. It's a wonder I completed my junior year, because toward the end, my concentration was gone. I stayed stoned right through finals.

On sober days, I scanned all of the newspapers looking for a job. I got a job out in Deer Park, Long Island as an electrical wire technician for a company that wired the machines used for making computer chips. I made a good salary to start. I was the only woman in my department, and was lucky to have a really fair boss. His name was Gary. He had curly blonde hair and walked with a limp because one of his legs were shorter than the other. I played basketball with my co-workers during lunch breaks and sometimes Gary would don his skates, grab a hockey stick and practice slamming the puck into the goal.

Things went pretty well at work. I followed the electrical blueprints, wired the machines properly and came in on weekends for special projects. I saved enough money to buy a used car because traveling from the Bronx, where I was now living, to Deer Park was no joke. Within six months, the Bronx electrical engineering department of a New

York Utility had hired me, so now my morning drive to work was shorter.

I got serious with this West Indian girl from St Croix named Cinnamon, that I met back in college. She worked downtown in the garment district as a receptionist. We rented a place in the most drug-infested part of the Bronx near Fordham road and the Major Deegan Expressway, because it was cheap. We were using as much coke as we were making money. I drank an equal amount of beer to level out the cocaine high and to keep my heart from beating out of my chest.

Cinnamon went to Manor College in the Bronx, not far from where we used to cop our drugs. I continued to work in the electrical engineering department and after work I picked her up from school. One night I went to pick her up and was taken by surprise because someone beat me to her.

She didn't know that I was coming and was surprised to see me. As I walked toward her, I had noticed t she was holding hands with some guy while he pushed his bike down the street. As I got closer she recognized me, and abruptly let his hand go. Cinnamon said good-bye to him, as he looked me up and down like I was in the way. As we started to walk home I asked her who he was. She said, nobody. I asked, "Well, why were you holding hands with a nobody?" She said, "Oh, he likes me, but I told him I was with someone."

I wasn't feeling that answer so shortly after that I started to drift away from her. Some nights I stayed out all night getting high, and some nights she didn't come home from school. In my mind she and the guy looked too snug and comfortable not to be having sex with each other. One day I took off from work and the guy called our home.

I asked him why he was calling in the daytime if he knew she was at work. He said, "I'll call her when I want." "No you won't, because she is with me," I said, and continued to tell him that if he held the phone a moment, I'd get her on the three-way so she could tell him that herself. Well, I got her on the phone and I said, "Tell this knuckle head that you don't want him calling here because you are with me."

There was silence on her end of the line. I said, "Tell him to stop calling here." She said nothing. She dissed me. I knew then that she was Bi-sexual and now I felt sick to my stomach. He said in a voice of satisfaction, "I told you she won't stop me from calling."

I was enraged and she and I argued. And we argued some more. The thought of her with him was driving me crazy. I kept envisioning their bodies together in bed and them going through the motions. I had to drink and do more coke to keep from killing her. I chose to get stoned because I was weak and embarrassed about that phone call. While I spent more time over at my neighbor Maritza's house getting high, Cinnamon began to hang out with a girl named CeeCee in Jersey.

The final straw came when Cinnamon left me this message on the answering machine. "Conscious, I'm not coming home tonight. I'm going to go to work from Jersey. Hope you are having fun wherever you are." Then I heard a voice, apparently from another extension. It said, "Fuck her. You don't have to explain where you are and what you are doing tomorrow. Fuck dat bitch. Hang up my phone, Cinnamon." I finally had enough. I found out Cinnamon had found a new woman. Now Cinnamon had him, her and me. Damn, that bitch got around.

I went crazy and began packing my clothes, dishes and all. Maritza's husband got me two supermarket shopping carts and I rolled my stuff down the block to my friend Maggie's house. She had an extra room that I could stay in because her son was away in the military. I left Cinnamon with one fork, one knife, a spoon, a plate, and a can of beans.

Hurt and pressed for time, I needed to stall her at work, so I called her and said, "Hi honey, I got your message, is everything okay?" I knew they didn't realize the machine had recorded all of the conversation I heard. "I want to make things up to you," I said, "I'm going to pick you up after work. If I'm running a little late, stand there and wait for me out front." I never showed and when she walked into the house later that night, she looked for me and thought we had been robbed. Later that month, I found an apartment in the Bronx near Yankee Stadium. It was all down hill from there.

What happened to you, what went wrong? You had every opportunity in life.

I know. I was a girl who had every reason in the world to succeed, and every opportunity, but instead I had chosen to fail. I gave up on life after that relationship. I headed for the grimy, dark side of life. I took the easy way out, drugs and alcohol.

So how did you deal with your pain?

I sniffed so much coke that it began to burn a hole from one side of my nasal passage to another. I spent most of the time getting high by myself and thinking about my miserable life. I'd buy coke from this guy named Keeco. There were countless nights of going back and forth to his drug spot and spending crazy money until daylight.

As far out as I was, I remember looking at the crackheads in the middle of the night as if they were an entirely different species, members of the land of the walking dead. I remember saying, "Damn, look at them. If I ever get caught up in the crack game then it would be all over, my last straw. I would have reached rock bottom." I vowed to myself that it would never happen. Little did I know I was already at the bottom, staying up all night, taking supposedly sobering showers and heading out to design electrical blueprints for a mall or a new housing development. Who was I fooling?

Unaware of my cocaine addiction, my friend, Dana, offered me an electrical job wiring her house. I was a functional addict and couldn't stop getting high long enough to do the job, though. Her career as Queen Latifah, recording artist, had brought her money and fame. She had bought a new house in New Jersey and asked me to wire the lights in her indoor swimming pool. I was so out of it that I told her that I couldn't do the job, but I could hook her up with an electrician who could. I was too busy wearing myself out with that "White Powder." I'd even caught pneumonia and had to be hospitalized. My spirit was empty inside. I thought I needed someone to fill me up, but it was me I needed. I needed to find me, but that wasn't going to happen until I hit rock bottom. And that's exactly where I was headed, to an ungodly, vicious, rock bottomless pit. A place where men worshiped twenty-four karat gold Saint Lazarus figures. A place where they worshipped the charm not because it represented a saint, but because, it was apart of the standard gear worn by their kind.

LAZ

Most thugs in this game,

Wear this Saint on their chains.

Wearing saints wearing charms,

Slinging drugs word is bond.

Give me strength clear my shame,

Back from death's where he came.

Save my life, get out this game,

Take off this charm, and make a change.

Figured out, what's his name?

Lazarus the Risen Saint.

I hadn't seen Justeen since we were kids. I had been thinking about her a lot while I was in the hospital, so when I came home I asked my sister had she seen Justeen. My sister said, "Yeah she's selling coke out of these apartments on Saint Nicholas, go over there and see her."

She was beautiful as ever with almond-shaped eyes and long, jet-black wavy hair. She was nutmeg-complexioned with a smile that could light up a room. She had a slim waist, thick thighs and a perfect round ass. You could tell she was a smoker, but to me it didn't matter because the first thought that came to my mind when I saw her was that she would provide me with everything I was lacking in a mother, a sister, a lover and a business partner. She would fill all the gaps for me, but there was one person in the way.

She ran a crackhouse and her drugs were supplied by a childhood friend who was now her drug connect. She sold drugs and rented out different rooms for people to use for sex, drugs, whatever. Her ex-man named Spanky with whom she was no longer intimate, stayed at the house with her when he wasn't out on one of his drug binges. She said Spanky was soft and for me not to worry about him. At one time he was a big heroin dealer, but one day he took a hit of the "glass dick" and became one of her best customers. That crack cocaine turned strong men into punks and made them stoop to the lowest levels just for a hit. So that's what I planned to give him, a hit to get out of my way so that I could make my money.

So you just made your move
and set up shop?

Yeah basically, it only took me one more visit before Justeen and I planned to become partners.

Spanky saw how Justeen and I got tight quickly so he backed off. He also saw that I was young, good-looking, influencing, and had money and drugs. I maintained arrogance and intimidation with the customers from the beginning so I could set my reputation on the scene. It's a type of arrogance you maintain when you are holding drugs over someone's head.

I gave Spanky one room in the back of the apartment to run his show while I rented out the front room, kitchen, bathroom and the closets for the crack smokers and dope shooters.

One day while we were sitting around in the apartment waiting for customers, this guy that looked like a "black Ken doll" with huge shoulders came in. He wore a derby, a mink jacket with a hood, and thick 24k gold iced-out Saint Lazarus charms dangling from thick gold chains. Following close behind him was this crackhead woman. As it turns out, it was Bishop, one of my friends from childhood. He was one of the kids I played hide-and-go-seek with in the backyards around the way. "Oh shit," he said laughing. "Yo, you getting money up in here?" "No doubt nigga, wusup" I said. "I thought you was in college playing ball and going to class with your preppy Izod Locaste shirts and your penny loafers." "Not no more." "Yeah I see that. It looks like you done traded all that shit in for those baggy Fubu jeans, that NY Yankees baseball hat and them Timberlands huh?" "Yeah, yeah so what, I did all that, and now I'm doing this. So, wasup nigga?" "Yeah Justeen told me you was bringing in a lot of money and you was keeping shit straight around here." "True, true." "So you wanna take this shit to the next level or what?" "Yeah as long as I get paid." "Aight. I want you to set up shop on our old block at your grandmother's house." "Yeah I been to the house a couple of times and Uncle Mickey got a lil flow going on in the block, but it could be better." "Yeah I know and Yo, the Latinos is clocking big dough on our old block. I want us to get a piece of that action. Yo, I already talked to Mickey, he will hold down the first floor, second floor, and the basement. Y'all movin into the house on the third floor, and yo, I want you to run that shit just like you did this shit, and no muthafuckin shorts you hear me?" "What about this shit here?" "Spanky is gonna hold this shit down but I want you to check on this nigga everyday to make sure my fuckin paper is right. Here take a look at this." He threw his knapsack in my direction. "Before you open that... What is the best way to keep your shit safe in a crackhouse?" He asked. "You sit on it." I responded. "Well, sit on that." And that's what I did. I sat on this knapsack stuffed with cocaine and money. "We gonna make moves in the morning, but I wanna party and get my dick sucked by this shorty first so keep clockin money. Somebody at the door." "Do your thing Bish, Justeen get the door."

As the woman sucked his dick, I used a razor blade to cut up the crack that sat in a big pile on a mirror on my lap. After I cut the crack into small pieces I stuffed them into little bottles and then stuffed all of the bottles into a small pouch. I was now prepared for my next batch of sales.

I watched as Bishop got "head." It was common for me to be in the room while girls took care of their business. There was no shame in their game as long as they got paid. They didn't care if the Pope was in the room watching.

The girl doing the sucking was like a lot of women and men who showed up, on a mission to get high. After a while, you know who comes to the door with money to buy and who comes in to give "head" or trade sex for drugs. Most of them are all strung out, disheveled, ragged, and begging from the start, but some try to maintain their composure and look like they are in control. Those are the ones who will try to maintain some dignity by requiring that the guy wash his penis or wear a condom. They were all sizes and colors from White to Black, Chinese to Latina.

Justeen's father Uncle Mickey was handsome and light skinned. He had a medium build with high cheekbones, light brown eyes and a "Blow out" haircut. He looked like this New York City DJ named Red Alert without the freckles. Uncle Mickey lived in his mother's house on the same block as Aunt Regina, right across the street. I remembered playing there as a child and Uncle Mickey giving me chess lessons on Sundays.

He was another one who used to sling dope and then one day took a hit of the glass dick and got hooked. The only difference was he was a crackhead who lived with his mother in a big house and was clocking crazy dollars, by selling girls in the house and renting rooms out. Uncle Mickey was about 60 years old, always had coke and always had his dick in some girl's mouth. The house was big with a lot of rooms. Bishop made arrangements for Uncle Mickey to continue to clock dollars while we took the top part of the house and clocked too. We split the house in two.

Where was your grandmother?
Did she know what was going
on?

Not really, she just knew there was a lot of traffic.

We called grandma Mrs. Phillips. She was about 84 years old and lived on the first floor. She spent most of her time sitting in her favorite chair looking out the front window. When people rang the bell we had to open the door quickly for them to either run upstairs, or downstairs before she came out to see who was there. That shit was funny sometimes because she used to ask, "Who just came in the house?" and we used to say, "Nobody." Sometimes she would wait 15 minutes and then raid us with her flashlight. But we worked around her.

We ultimately converted the seven-bedroom house into our little business, a crack den and house of ill repute. We rented out rooms for $30 an hour to guys who used it for sex with crackheads. We called the basement The Bat Cave. It was pitched black and quiet down there accept for the crackling sound of crack burning on the red-hot amber screens, held by the glass dick.

We kept a supply of shaker bottles, baking soda, lighters, razor blades, mirrors, glass dicks, girls, plenty of coke, and what we called a tech. A tech was a thin metal rod, usually taken from an umbrella with a flat tip, which we used to scrape the residue that accumulated along the walls in the glass dick. When the crack heads cooked their cocaine and reduced it to its base, they'd end up with these small nuggets in the shaker bottle. When it's cooked and ready to smoke, the jiggling sounds like you are shaking a marble back and forth inside of an empty mayonnaise bottle. That's when the crackheads would start saying "Your jiggling baby, beam me up Scotty."

*So when did you take your first
hit off the so-called glass dick?*

I never hit the pipe.

Yeah right.

My first taste of crack was when my cousin put her mouth over mine and then blew it into me. It was called a "shotgun." She would inhale the crack and then blow the smoke into my mouth. The first time it happened I got really horny. I looked at her like I was ready to jump her bones, and she said, "No don't even think about it." And smiled. I said "Why you say that?" "Cause you look like you ready to do something real nasty to me." "You must be thinking just like me then, nasty. Come here." I gave her a long intense kiss. Then we got busy.

Justeen and I would spend hours getting high, cooking coke, bagging coke, and counting money. She was the balance in the house. She was gentle, patient and kind. She was always getting on me about being so intimidating with customers. And when I was with my boys, Nappy and Diesel, I was always ready to bust somebody's shit. But, Justeen could calm me down in a second. All she had to do was run her fingers across the back of my neck and smile. I would relax instantly.

When customers weren't occupying the rooms in our house, they were kept locked. The girls were allowed to stay in a room in the basement, sort of a holding area until new customers came. They got high, talked and laughed until the bell rang. They knew then that we had a customer with money or someone with a hit of crack, so they perked up and fixed their stems. Once the guys came in, they would select a girl and be dispatched to a vacant room to make us some money. They paid up front. When the hour was up, I'd bang on the door. Either they would leave or I would collect more money, and give out more drugs and condoms. I was the supplier. If the guy wanted a new girl, I'd supply that too.

Sometimes women would come and rent rooms. I would get them either a guy or another girl. But, who was I to abuse them and dispatch any man or woman to a room? Who gave me the right? I thought I was a big shot, but I wasn't, I had become a monster with a deadened soul. I began to misuse and abuse these women the way that I had been used as a child. The abuse cycle was in full swing. I had become my predator.

Inside, I knew that I should have cared about these women and what I was doing. But it was business. It was as if I was in front of Madison Square Garden hailing cabs for a line of people. I was merely an agent to get them where they wanted to go. I mean, if they didn't catch the cab here they would catch it somewhere else. Either way, they were going to take the trip.

Bishop got busted at the airport with money and coke so our money got short. The feds had been watching him for months, people said. For big money my cousin started renting out the whole third floor for cocaine and cash, usually a couple of hundred for a couple of hours. Dealers would use our spot to cook their coke and bag the crack. Nobody got in without a good reason and I kept a gun at the door.

I started running with a crew that would stick up first-comers down the block in the hallways after they copped coke from the Latino dealers. After we got away, we went to the store to get forty ounces of beer and then walked right past them and into my house to sell their shit, and get high out of our minds.

My crew snatched the pockets off anyone vulnerable-looking; mostly people leaving the building, having purchased large amounts of crack.

We figured they really couldn't go to the cops. How could they explain being robbed of crack in a crack infested building in this neighborhood? If we didn't harass them, one of our rivals on the block would harass them before they could get to the corner.

I watched my friend Monique snatch the coke dealer's stash on a regular basis. Monique was a short, dark-skinned girl with a big smile, but her entire upper row of teeth was missing except the two on the side. Her hair was always nappy and covered by a bandana, but she always had on a new halter-top and tight ass jeans that she boosted out of the stores on Broadway. She had been in the drug game for ten years before me and she knew my mom, so she was like family. She ran with a posse who would buy small amounts of drugs from dealers to find out where they hid their stash. Later they went back to rip them off. On other occasions, someone from their group would go in the building during a buy and hide out until closing time then take all they could and sneak out of a back window. The dealers may have suspected that Monique was involved, but they never caught her in the act. I took matters to the extreme. I suppose I had a bit of a death wish. But, I didn't care. I would case out the block and watch the dealers for part of the day to catch their patterns. When they shut down their operations, I raided all of their stashes and took everything I could before they knew what hit them. It was easy for me because I knew every back yard and rooftop in the neighborhood since I was a kid. These were the same yards and houses I ran through throwing rocks and wreaking havoc with Bishop.

Nobody liked these new drug dealers because they acted like they owned our block. They made the most money of all the hustlers and were cocky and flashy with motorcycles, gold, diamonds and big leather money belts. Their big-time suppliers made it known that nobody was to cross them or take their shit and that made me all the more defiant and determined when I didn't have any coke.

I thought I was stuck in that cruddy life. I started getting fever blisters on my lips, getting real thin, and my skin started changing shades from smoking crack. I started to get the shakes if I didn't have a drink of liquor or a forty-ounce of beer to start the day off. I began to become addicted to what I was doing, and I thought there was no way out. The alcohol kept telling me that I was bold, and the cocaine kept calling me, so I kept running to it. The combination of the two would soon kill me.

Hitting the drug dealer's stash became like a fix for me. I got a thrill out of getting away with it. I was good with a key. That's what we called a crow bar. I could skillfully use it to pry open doors and windows. I thought I was invincible. Drugs will do that to you, especially crack cocaine. And at this point I was using as much as I was selling.

Most of the time I rolled with my boys Diesel and Nappy. Nappy was big with a big Afro and a quick temper. His favorite line was, "You heard what he said break yourself." The next thing you knew Nappy had knocked the guy to the floor with an open hand slap. His hands were that big. Diesel was quiet with huge muscles. You could see his bulging biceps, forearms and chest through his coat in the winter. They both were about 6'2", but Diesel was bigger. The three of us were straight up thugs always looking to bum rush someone. They looked out for me and I looked out for them. Everything was rolling pretty well until that last heist, though.

I knew that I was burning a bridge I would never be able to cross again. But I didn't care. It was like I was giving myself an ultimatum; either keep taking those stashes, smoking and get myself killed or get myself together.

I was headed back to the house after a night of partying with my crew. It was noon and I had about $30 left in my pocket, more than enough to buy a gram of coke. As I approached my block, I noticed that all of the coke dealers were running out of the buildings and the block was crawling with cops. Police trucks were parked in the street with lights flashing. Police were harassing everyone in sight.

I had just enough time to run into my house, get the key (the crowbar), run up to the fifth floor of their building and hit their stash. I had had previous opportunities to case their spot really well. I knew where they kept the gun, the coke, the crack and the money. It was too good to be true. The place was empty since coke dealers were scattered like roaches, and the police were my cover.

I reached the door to their apartment and to my surprise they had ran out the building so fast for fear of getting arrested that they left the apartment unlocked. I went straight for the stash and took half a kilo of coke, several ounces of crack and a bag full of money. I didn't have enough time to find the gun. I was in and out.

I left the building and walked right past the police, who had the coke dealers lined up on the walls and facedown on the hot concrete. I had put the crowbar back inside my pant leg and stashed everything else inside the waist of my pants. I went two doors down to our house, ran up the stairs and told my cousin and uncle what I had just done.

"Why did you come straight here?" Uncle Mickey screamed. It was pretty dumb of me because five minutes later, two of the coke dealers came busting in our door and put a gun to my chest. "Where's our shit?" Rico said. I said, "What shit?" I looked at them like they were crazy. They weren't completely sure, and they hadn't seen me do it. They may have seen me go in and come out, but that wouldn't have been unusual since on occasion I would buy from them and that was my intention that day. They had to be 100 percent sure before they shot me. Besides they wanted their shit back so they wouldn't have to explain to the big bosses what happened during their shift. "You took our shit," Rico said in a thick Spanish accent. His partner, Manny, said little. He was like the silent enforcer.

"I didn't take your shit," I screamed back. "There were other people in the building, too."

Uncle Mickey was shaking like Jello. I backed up into a bedroom with my hands in the air, while he made a move for his shotgun. Manny and Rico started to get nervous. The cops were right outside and Mrs. Phillips had the front door wide open saying, "Who just came in? And don't say nobody came in because I saw them. I'm gonna call the cops. They are right outside. I am tired of this in-and-out mess." If they shot me, it would draw too much attention and there was no way for them to get out of our house without getting caught. Uncle

Mickey told them that I wouldn't be stupid enough to come right next door after I had hit their stash. But I had done just that. I was slipping. The crack had me wide open making stupid moves. He told them that I didn't have the drugs and convinced them to walk down the steps to the front door. As they got to the bottom of the steps, I looked over the banister and they looked up and whispered, "You got our shit don't you? Watch your back." When they got to the front door, they politely said hello to grandma and she went off on them. "I knew I saw you guys come in here! What are you doing in here now?" "Get out before I call the cops on you, and they deport all your asses back to your own country."

By the time Uncle Mickey came back up the stairs I was pouring some of the coke and some of the crack on a mirror for him. That was his cut for looking out for me. Then I stuffed the two huge baggies of coke back down my pants and jumped out the second-floor window, over two fences, down a 10-foot wall to a basement and up the basement steps to the next block. When I got to the other side, to safety, I let out a rebel yell up to a window and said, "Aye yo, it's on!" I had reached my safe house. Monique came to the window and said, "Yo, wus up?" I said, "Yo let me in son, it's on." She said, "Aight I'll be right down. Step into the hallway get off the stoop before someone sees you." I went upstairs and sat in the kitchen and told her what I did. When she saw how much I had, she said, "Now you know you can't go back to the block right?" I said, "Yeah I know. Now cook some of this shit and let's see how it tastes. You done? Now give me a shotgun." And she did. After I came down off the hit, we sent someone to get me a cab with tinted windows so I could get out of the neighborhood. I hit her off with some coke and then "Got to steppin."

I knew that I had reached a point of no return. I could feel it. I had never had butterflies before. I was never nervous when I hit their stash. But this time I was and by the next day the coke dealers had an All Points Bulletin (APB) out on my ass.

Even the threat of death didn't stop me, though. I knew I had to lay low, but I still couldn't stay away from Justeen and she didn't know where I was. I was tightly wound and started traveling from block to block by way of the backyards. Everybody I knew started saying, "Yo Conscious, the dealers are looking for you. They are beating up every girl who looks like you with a baseball bat." But, nothing seemed to move me. I must have been on a death wish.

The next day in the wee hours of the morning, I snuck in the house through the backyard window. I made it up to our apartment on the third floor where Justeen was. It had a fireplace, kitchen, two tall windows facing the infamous backyard (my escape route) and a closet. There was a nice couch, a queen-size bed and a 20-inch TV with ghetto cable. (You pay for the box and get the cable free.) She had been awake for days and I hadn't slept all night. We were both wired and coked out. I spent the rest of the morning trying to come down, by making love to her until she fell asleep. I was still half-asleep lying on top of her when I heard this voice behind me. I froze. I just knew I was dead.

The voice said, "Get up and leave this place. You have work to do." I whipped my head around and saw that no one was there. This was the same voice I had heard as a child, when I had conversations with God. A chill ran through my body. This time the voice told me that I would be stricken with an illness, but would not be affected until my work was done. I got up right then, got dressed and left the same way I came in. I thought they had finally caught me, but it wasn't them. It was God saving me. I was at the end of my rope. Justeen still asleep, didn't know what had happened. I didn't either, but I knew I had to go.

I still had drugs left from the heist. I gave most of them away and finished the rest at a crackhouse in a different neighborhood. After the drugs were all gone, I slept in the basement. Two days later, I woke up and walked 17 blocks to my sister's place. She had been begging me for three years to come stay with her and get out of the life I was leading. She was afraid for me. She had seen what crack had done to the whole neighborhood because she used to come there to try and get me to leave. She was a mother committed to providing a nice life for her three children. She had a job, a nice apartment and childhood friends who wanted me to be in their sober world.

On the walk there, I thought about the lecture I would get when I saw her. I thought about what I would say. It was 2 in the afternoon and the sun was beating down, but nothing like the heat I was walking away from.

I got to her door, took a deep breath and rang the doorbell. She opened the door, took one look at my face and said, "Are you finished now?"

I was dirty, skinny, my hair was short and uncombed with some huge fake jewelry on that was turning-all-kinds-of colors. My sister said her heart started to race. Even in our toughest times, broke or strung out, the women in my family kept their appearance together and didn't wear cheap jewelry.

She sent me to the bathroom, fed me and relaxed my hair. Later that evening my sister recommended that I check myself into some place for drug treatment. She had friends who had done a 12-month program and gotten themselves straightened out. She bought some toiletries and other things that I'd need when I arrived to register in this program.

I made it through the weekend sober and got on the "A" train to Far Rockaway, Queens to our intake facility. I had been in the streets for three years.

So how was it for you when
you first got here?

I stayed in the check-in center in Far Rockaway for a week until a bed became available at our facility in Parksville. It was a three-hour bus ride up here and as I rode on the bus I remember saying to myself "I am up here in this small hick town with all these big houses. How are they going to help me?" I mean, I was invincible. I could take on the world. But, I knew the world was catching up with me and I was tired. I was tired of getting high, tired of selling drugs, tired of selling women, tired of running the streets, tired of running from myself, tired of being hurt, tired of the violence, tired of my disguise, and just tired of being "*stuck*".

Ok lets wrap it up. I hope that each one of you has flushed out some or most of your pain, and I hope that you stay on your path to recovery. Everything that has been exposed within these four walls must remain here. We all have hurt and pain that drove us to use drugs and alcohol, and we have all done some ugly, foolish and degrading things for drugs. My solution to dealing with your past is to stop beating yourselves up and begin to build yourselves up. The most important thing that you need to know is that you realized that there was a serious problem. You surrendered to God and He led you here to Daytop for help. Please give thanks and praise

to God because without him
there would be no us.
Remember that the path to
recovery begins with change.

Getting Unstuck

15

It was a routine physical examination given when you're on your way out of a treatment program. They also routinely ask you whom you want present when you get results from the HIV test. I chose my close friend John.

I got the results from the HIV test on Friday. Allan had the weekend off from work. A week or two had gone by since the test and it had been in the back of my mind until they called me up to the HIV counselor's office. When they called me into the room there were three people in there; the HIV counselor, a counselor who was HIV Positive, and my friend John. I knew what the results were by the way that John dropped his head when I walked in. When presented with the positive results I handled it really calmly and told the HIV counselor that it would be ok. They all sat there in shock, and thought that I would break down and cry, but I didn't. I was prepared. They didn't know what I knew. If they did, they wouldn't have been confused by my response. At that moment, I realized that another part of my journey had been uncovered. I was finally faced with the sickness that was revealed to me by God months ago in that crackhouse.

From the window in the cafeteria I saw Allan when he returned to work on Monday. When he pulled up to the facility, the HIV counselor met him at the gate and informed him of my medical status. When he walked into the Pinnacle, he wouldn't make eye contact with me. I could see he was hurting. He was in so much pain that he turned around and walked back outside. He walked around in a circle, looking down at the ground, shaking his head as he smoked a cigarette. I followed him outside and said,

Allan, I owe you everything. You knew what needed to be done to help me breakthrough to my childhood. You covered every base possible. There was nothing you could have done for this. Nobody knew that this was there, not even me.

> *I know, but why you? I just wish I could have done something to prevent this from happening to you.*

I know. You probably wish you could have spared me of a whole lifetime of mess, but don't be crazy Allan, you made me go get tested so, pat yourself

on the back for that. Just imagine if I never got tested, or if I never came to Daytop. Allan, it was the unknowing (the repressed memory) that would have killed me. This I know. This I can live with.

After we were done talking we walked into the pinnacle together and Allan delivered the afternoon seminar. After Allan finished his seminar on sharing secrets and staying clean, he turned the floor over to me and said,

> *Family, Conscious has something very important to share with you.*

I began by thanking everybody for his or her support over the past year and when I disclosed my medical situation, people started to gasp for air and say oh no.

I went on to tell them every single personal thing that happened to me because I knew that it would help them. One of the sayings at Daytop is "You can't keep it unless you give it away." I believed that, so I continued, and as I looked around I saw people at the tables crying and some sitting forward on their chairs wanting to hear more. Two people who were angry with God had puddles of tears in their eyes as they said to me, "How could God do this to you?" I said,

I don't know. I never asked Him that question, but what I do know is that I have a purpose here, just like I know I heard a voice from God one night that saved my life. I accept God's plan for me.

Another person asked, "Do you know where you got it and when?"

Yes, from my cousin but I have not been able to confront her on it yet.

I know for sure that I was not HIV-Positive when I had pneumonia in the early 90s. After that time I had sex with one person, my cousin Justeen. When I found out my status on Friday I called home to ask my sister questions about how Justeen looked and how she was doing. To my surprise she told me that Justeen looked really sick and the rumor was that her ex-man Spanky was HIV-Positive. She said that they were both sick, but apparently my cousin was more advanced than he was. My sister thinks that

Justeen has AIDS. Funny, I never would have suspected my cousin had AIDS the whole time we were together. She looked fine to me, but that's the mistake a lot of us make. AIDS affects everybody's system differently. You could be in the full-blown stage with AIDS and still look healthy. Ironically, I made sure I didn't mess around with anybody but her because I always said I didn't want to contract AIDS from one of those crackheads. I slept with her exclusively and I got caught out there anyway.

Another curious person asked, "So how do you think you contracted the virus from her? I mean, I didn't know that girl to girl you could be infected. I thought that only man-to-man, woman-to-man, or man-to-woman you can be infected."

No, that is one of the biggest myths associated with transmittal of the virus and I am here to tell you that it can happen. It did happen. And now as I think back, I know exactly what I did with her to contract the virus.

Everybody in the room sat forward on their chairs.

Oral sex with open fever blisters on my mouth and finger penetration with open cuts on my fingers and hands. The cuts on my hands were caused by that glass dick constantly breaking, and other open wounds on my hands were caused by handling cocaine without any protection. After handling cocaine continuously, the chemicals chapped and cracked my hands, thus enabling the virus easy entrance into my system.

What made it worse was sometimes Justeen bled during finger penetration because my nails scratched and pierced the tissue lining along the walls of her vagina during rough sex. Do you know how many people give finger penetration and don't pay attention to the open cuts they have on their hands or fingers? It only takes one open cut on a finger to become vulnerable to the virus. Especially in the vagina because an infected vagina is filled with the fluid that carries the virus. If I ever get a chance to tell my story to the masses, I would make sure to address the electricians, the carpenters, the mechanics and all the people who use their hands to do work. I would tell them that they had better think twice before sticking their fingers or mouths in it, unless their fingers and mouths are protected the same way one protects a penis. And what about the lesbians who have sex during their menstrual cycle? They need to be real careful when coming in contact with their partners' blood. That goes for the heterosexual men as well. Those are the men that want to earn their "red wings" by having intercourse with their woman while she is on the "rag".

Justeen and I frequently had sex when she had her period. Just think of how the risk factor multiplies dramatically. You think you are having good sex because you feel horny during your period, but if you are unknowingly infected and unprotected, there is substantial risk.

And for the so-called two straight girls, who have a threesome with one guy, watch out. After you are done sexing him, you need to protect yourself when you start to sex each other. Don't think that you don't have to be as careful when you come in contact with that female because girl to girl, you can be, infected indeed.

My sister was right. I received a call from Justeen saying that she was very sick in the hospital and that Spanky was HIV positive. Allan immediately made arrangements for me to visit her. When I arrived at the hospital she looked very small and skeletal. I was in shock to see that her body had almost disappeared in the year that I had been gone. There was a pond in Central Park that she used to love to walk by; it was across the street from the hospital. I got her up out of the bed. But before we could get out the room, she held my face with her two little hands and started to kiss me and pull me back to her bed. I put my head down and started to cry. We both started to cry, the way we did when we met each other the first time. It was hard for me to stop but I had to. I had to be strong for both of us. I couldn't do it with her anymore because I had found myself and I was now strong. She thought that things would still be the same, but I tried to explain to her that what we did was not healthy, not good. I told her everything I had learned about myself and explained to her that what she really meant to me was safety. I asked her if there was something she wanted to share with me, and she did. She said that she too had been molested in that same house by our relatives and strangers who babysat her. Then she said that her T-Cell count was down to 3 and that she was taking AZT. That's when I told her about me being HIV-positive. As she sat back against her pillow, she looked out the window to the park across the street and tears rolled down her face. She said, "Oh my God what did I do to you?"

I didn't want to make her feel guilty by throwing this whole thing in her face, because what was done was done, and I knew she didn't have much time to live. We held hands as I took her for that walk by the pond in Central Park then, and on other occasions. She passed away six months later.

I knew that it was now time for me to leave the program and to start a new life for myself without my cousin. When I got home, I was healthy, mentally sound, hungry for success and most of all sober. The first job I landed was as a bouncer at a New York nightclub called "The Tunnel," where me and a detail of bodyguards were fortunate to have protected celebrities such as Aaliyah, Missy Elliot, Timberland, Magoo, Ginuwine, Fat Joe, Jay Z, Eve, Ja Rule, Big Pun and more. In time, I began to work at the "Palladium," "The Lime Light" and other various nightclubs. I even met "Marky" Mark Wahlberg the actor, who hired me to become his bodyguard during the premier of his hit movie, "Boogie Nights."

I was no longer tormented by my former lifestyle. I had conquered my fears and was now paving my future. It was all happening so fast, the next thing I knew I was on television. I couldn't wait to tell Allan.

See Allan, I knew God had a plan for me.

Why do you say that
Conscious?

Because God is slowly working me back into society.

So where are you staying?

I am staying at my sister's house in Harlem, and trying to feel my way around in life, to see where I fit in again.

You think you might want to
have some kids?

Nah, but I did meet a couple of guys and tried dating men. I even tried wearing a skirt, nails and lipstick.

How was it, did you give it a chance?

Yeah I gave it a chance, but I wasn't real comfortable with all that stuff. I quickly found that my attraction is still for woman. I find men attractive, but women really do it for me. I guess that's something that I can't change.

Don't worry, you don't have to change that unless you want to. You are a beautiful woman and any man would kill to be with you. You have come a long way Conscious. I witnessed you rescue that little girl inside of you and help her to grow emotionally. I have watched you work hard in therapy to transform from this young male thug into a beautiful young productive woman. Don't worry about your

sexuality, that will reveal itself,
just as everything else has.

I sat there absorbing all of Allan's affirmations. He always kept it real and helped me to see my progress.

So have you met any nice
ladies?

Yes, a couple. But I really like this half-Dominican half Puerto Rican woman the most. She has a three-year old son and lives in Brooklyn.

How long have you guys been
dating?

For a couple of weeks.

Does she know?

Yeah, I told her after about three weeks into the relationship.

So what did she say?

She started crying, then she told me that she needed a moment alone. I went for a walk and when I came back, she grabbed me and told me she loved me anyway and that she would be there for me until the end. She said that she was my soul mate and no matter what disease I had, we were gonna work through this.

That's cool so how do you feel about that?

I think that it's only fair to let your partner know about your medical situation. That knowledge gives them the opportunity to say whether or not they want to be with you.

You are absolutely right and as long as you stay honest with your partner, the more precautions you guys can take to prevent anymore transmission of the virus. So what kind of work are you doing? Did you land a job yet?

Yeah, you won't believe this Allan!

What?

For the first couple of months when I came home I worked as a bodyguard for celebrities.

Really?

Yes, and then I applied for an internship program at a television network and was accepted. Ironically, I was asked to work on a TV show that was being produced about gays and transsexuals. I said to myself, I know a little something about that. I asked the producers if they knew why people cross-dressed or become gay and they stared at me with blank faces. They were clueless. So, I gave them some answers from my own experience. After I finished working on the show and coaching the producers I moved on to the technical department where I wired everything in the place from the computers down to the digital equipment. They were going to hire me at the end of the internship, but something else came up.

What?

A talk show.

Really?

Yeah, you are not going to believe who I've been working with for the past couple of months Allan, Guess who!

Who? Tell me.

Queen Latifah.

A woman at the network named Trish was so proud of my work during my internship that she told the executive producer of the Queen Latifah Show about me.

When Trish told me that she was going to set me up with a job working for Latifah I started buggin out. I couldn't believe it. I told her, that I knew Queen Latifah and she started buggin too, because she knew Conny Thermol, the executive producer of

Latifah's talk show at Telepictures Productions. Conny was looking for an executive assistant so Trish set up the interview.

Trish and Conny worked together on that television show called EXTRA, and she knew that I would live up to Conny's expectations as an executive assistant.

Great how was the interview?

When I got to Conny's office on the 32nd floor of that big building across the street from Radio City Music Hall, I was nervous as hell, but when I met Conny she made me feel comfortable. We talked about my internship and how Latifah and I used to play ball together in the Village. When I left her office, I just knew I had that job.

Allan this was a spiritual moment for me. Latifah and my paths had come around full circle, but this time I was proper and free of drugs and negative influences. I knew that my soul was clean and that I needed to make a positive first impression to prove that I was clean for good.

Two weeks later, my friend Noodie told me that Latifah was having another annual benefit basketball game. Latifah had developed a scholarship fund, in the name of her deceased brother Lancelot H. Owens, to help inner the city youth enter college. So I invited Conny to the game. When Latifah walked into the gym she was rushed by a group of kids and adults for autographs. I was standing off to the far corner near the bleachers when she saw me for the first time in three years. The whole time I was out in the streets she kept asking Cinnamon if I was okay and if anyone had seen me. When she looked at me, I know she must have been thinking, "When did Conscious make her way back from the land of the dead?" As she walked towards me she immediately hugged me and said "Wow, Conscious, back to life. Damn, where have you been? You look great. You alright?" I said, "We'll talk, We'll talk. Dana smiled and said, "Okay, cool, we'll kick it later."

She was right, I had been brought back to life the same way St. Lazarus had. I was once among the walking dead and some how God miraculously helped me back to life. I didn't even try to explain then. I knew we would have plenty of time to catch up once we got to her music studio.

Conny told her that she was interested in making me a part of the show. If I know Dana, she was saying to herself, "Conscious must have really gotten her shit together to impress this Exec." Dana said, "Yeah Conny, good pick," and put her arm around my shoulder. "Conscious is my buddy, we go way back she's an excellent pick for an executive assistant."

That conversation confirmed my position. I'm in there, Allan.

> *Good, good you seem really excited about that. Have you been taking care of your health?*

Yeah.

> *When was the last time you been to the doctor.*

Two weeks ago. I had my T-Cell count checked.

How does it look?

It looks good. My viral load is under 10,000 and my T-Cell count is about 336.

So does your doctor want you to start medication yet?

No, he said I didn't need to start medication because I am doing really good and my vitals are stable.

So how do you feel?

I feel like a million bucks Allan.

You sure?

Yeah, look at me, I feel great Allan. Stop worrying.

Okay, okay. So what else is new?

Everything is falling into place for me.

Why do you say that?

I got a call from Oxygen Media this week.

Oxygen huh? Isn't that Oprah Winfrey's new network?

Yeah, one of the hosts from the show titled "She-Commerce" is going out on maternity leave and they need someone to fill in until she comes back.

Really, so how did they pick you?

They were asking around and auditioning people and then one day an employee at Telepictures Productions suggested they contact me. When the Oxygen Network contacted me they said that I had a great soul that would bring life to their show.

What! So you up to it?

Yeah, I audition on Friday and if they like me, I go into the studio to tape next week.

So, who will you interview first?

I will interview Laila Ali, the boxer on Wednesday, then the following Tuesday I interview rapper MC Lyte and actress Tischina Arnold from the sitcom "Martin."

Oh yeah?

Yeah Ltye has a clothing line called Lyte Wear and Tischina has a bandana line called China Moon Rags. They will be promoting their products on the show so I am going to make sure I help to "plug" them both.

Conscious I am so proud of you. Come here give me a big hug.

I love you, Allan.

I love you, too. Keep up the
good work because you will be
amazing.

When I get the gig can you come watch my first show Allan?

Yeah, give me the address to
the studio. I'll be there in the
front row.

Thanks Allan. Thank you for helping me recover my memory and thank you for helping me to break that sick cycle of sexual abuse and drug addiction.

Don't thank me, you did all the
hard work.

Well thanks to you, now all I have to do is continue to work hard, stay alive, stay sober, and remain "Unstuck".

Alpha

THANK YOU'S

MY PUBLISHER; GOD, DR. BAILEY, LYNN, CHARELL,
APRIL, WAKI, PEACHES, ANTHONY, MIKE, MY
ATTORNEYS; WILFREDO BENITEZ, AND ERIC
PENNINGTON, MILDRED, JOANNA SANTIAGO, ALLAN
BENJAMIN, MARGAUX, CHYNA, BAMBUE, DUCE, CATHY
CHERMOL, QUEEN LATIFAH, QUEEN PENN, LL COOL J,
CHIVON DEAN CEO RUFF RYDERS, LB, THE FLAVOR
UNIT RECORDS FAMILY, TRA` RENEE FROM WBLS FM,
ANANDA LEWIS, MONICA JOSEPH, TARA, FUNKMASTER
FLEX, RAQIYAH, THE SOURCE, VENUS MAGAZINE,
OXYGEN MEDIA, RENEE, HBO SOUL POETRY,
TELEPICTURES PRODUCTIONS, NEW LINE CINEMA,
RACHELLE AND JEFF CHRISTIE, IN LOVING MEMORY OF
KENNY GREEN, KAREN HUNTER, MALAIKA ADERO,
CHARNITA AND KEITH SWEAT, RITA, TEREASA,
WEATHERSPOON, MONIFAH, MC-LYTE, TACHINA, MOON
MADISON THE PROMOTER, STARR, TRE, LISA S, TAMMY,
KEVIN, DEE, DIONDRA, TRACY POTTS, ROC BUNCE,
NYJGA GREEN, STACEY BATTLES, THE ENTIRE TUNNEL
SECURITY TEAM, NOODIE, JAMELLA, IN LOVING
MEMORY OF LYNN GIFFITH, SAUNDRA, PJ, IONE, JACKIE
FARNAN, KALIMAH, MRS. JENKINS, ALINDA, LO,
CRYSTAL, LAUNCY, THE NEW YORK SHARKS WOMEN'S
FOOTBALL TEAM, ALLYSON, ALANA, SPIVEY, MARLENE
THE ENTIRE WEST 4TH STREET PLAYGROUND BBALL
SQUAD, SURROB, TONY, NECHELLE, UBEU, CHERYL, MY
NEW FRIENDS; TERRIE WOODS, ROCHELLE, JABBAR,
RAHEEM KIA, ORY, SHAMONE, STEPHANIE, STELLA,
VIVIAN, TAKIA, DINO, PHIL GAZZILLO, MIKE BEHRENS,
DENISE FROM STAPLES, LISA FROM KINKOS, MICHELLE
AND ALL OF MY SUPPORTERS. I LOVE YOU!
And If I missed you, I love YOU too!

"Let me be the sacrifice. Let me be the example. Don't
say nobody told you so, and guard your kids!"*Conscious*

THE MUSIC THAT I LISTEN TO WHILE I WRITE.

DMX…. "SLIPPIN"

BONE THUGS "CROSSROADS"

MAXWELL.."THIS WOMAN'S WORK"

TONI BRAXTON….."BREATH AGAIN" AND "HOW MANY WAYS?" AND "I LOVE ME SOME HIM"

JESSIE POWELL…"YOU"

KENNY LATTIMORE…."ALWAYS REMEMBER"

METHOD MAN AND MARY J BLIGE… "ALL THAT I NEED"

MARIAH CAREY'S.."BUTTERFLY ALBUM"

JON B'S 1ST ALBUM

BEE BEE AND CEE CEE WINANS…"DON'T CRY FOR ME"

JAMES INGRAM.."WHATEVER WE IMAGINE"

ALEXANDER O'NEAL.."SUNSHINE"

MICHAEL JACKSON.."KEEP THE FAITH", "WILL YOU BE THERE?" AND "THE MAN N THE MIRROR"

GLENN JONES "IN YOU" AND "LOVE IS FOREVER"

CHICO DEBARGE "LONG TIME NO SEE ALBUM"

To **Whitney Houston, Bobby Brown, Robert Downey Jr**. I hope that my book helps you to understand how to unbury your pain. And to **DMX,** I share the same pains, demons, and happiness that you write about in your lyrics.

Recommended HIV/AIDS Web Sites

Aegis
http://www.aegis.com

AIDS Clinical Trials Information Service
http://www.actis.org

The Body
http://www.thebody.com

Centers for Disease Control and Prevention
http://www.cdc.gov/nchstp/hiv_aids/pubs/facts.htm

CDC National Prevention Information
http://www.cdcnpin.org

Community Research Initiative on AIDS
http://www.criany.org

DHHS AIDS Treatment Information Service
http://www.hivatis.org

HIV/AIDS Glossary (English)
http://www.sfaf.org/treatment/glossary

HIV/AIDS Glossary (Spanish)
http://aidsinfonyc.org/network/lared/glosterm.html

HIV Insite
http://hivinsite.ucsf.edu

HIVline
http://www.hivline.com

The John Hopkins AIDS Service
http://www.hopkins-aids.edu

Medscape
http://www.medscape.com/home/topics/AIDS/AIDS.html

National AIDS Education and Training Centers
http://www.ucsf.edu/warmline/aetc.html

National Library of Medicine
http://www.sis.nlm.nih.gov/aidswww.htm

National Pediatric AIDS Network
http://www.npan.org

POZ Magazine
http://www.poz.com

Project Inform
http://www.projectinform.org

If you have questions or comments about NATIP, please send e-mail to PSAVINO@CAREGROUP.HARVARD.EDU Project Manager, or phone NATIP at (617) 667-5520.

Get your questions answered

Center for Disease Control

AIDS Hotline 1-(800)-342-2437

(*) www.cdc.gov

Get tested

HIV Home Test Kits (Approved by FDA however consult a physician for counseling first. Also check with your local Health department for free testing.)

(*) www.homeaccess.com

Help a Kid

Teen Alcohol abuse and addiction
(*) www.focusas.com/alcohol.html

In the Mix Alcohol Abuse
(*) www.pbs.org/mix/alcohol_index.html

Kids-in-crisis
(*) www.geocities.com/heartland/bluffs/5400

Help a Survivor

Incest survivors Anonymous
(*) www.csutk.cdu/~bartley/other/isa.html

(*) All Internet addresses are subject to change.
If so check with your yellow pages for local listing in your area.

Questions and answers from Beth Isreal Deaconess Center, 330 Brookline Avenue, Libby Rm. 342, Boston, MA 02215

Phone (617) 667-5520 Fax (617) 667-2885 FAXBACK (800) 399-AIDS

http://www.natip.org/index.htm

How can I find out if I am infected with HIV?

A blood test to detect the antibody to HIV is available through your doctor or local clinic. Because there is a delay between the time you become HIV-infected and the development of antibodies, you should be tested six months following your last high risk behavior. If you are concerned about the HIV antibody results becoming part of your medical record, you can be tested through an anonymous test site or by using a home test kit. Check with your local or state public health department for more information about testing options.

What should I do if I am diagnosed with HIV infection?

Before being tested for HIV antibody, you should have a plan for what you would do if the results are positive. Anxiety, anger, denial, and depression are common reactions. You should discuss the way you feel with friends, family, or mental health professionals.

It is important to understand that HIV infection is by no means a "death sentence" and that people typically live for many years after the diagnosis. There are now very effective drugs available for treatment of HIV infection and for prevention of complications. You may benefit from medical therapy even if you have no symptoms. Make an appointment with your primary care provider, or, if you do not have one, ask your testing site or local HIV/AIDS service organization for a referral to a doctor experienced in treating HIV disease.

What does AIDS mean?

AIDS stands for **acquired immunodeficiency syndrome**, which is a designation for the more advanced stages of HIV disease, established by the Centers for Disease Control and Prevention. To meet criteria for an AIDS diagnosis, you must have one of the following: 1) current or past history of severe opportunistic disease (for example, PCP, toxo, KS, cervical cancer, MAC, CMV, tuberculosis); 2) HIV dementia (memory impairment) or wasting syndrome (involuntary weight loss); or 3) CD4 count less than 200/mm3.

How can I find out if I am infected with HIV?

A blood test to detect the antibody to HIV is available through your doctor or local clinic. Because there is a delay between the time you become HIV-infected and the development of antibodies, you should be tested six months following your last high risk behavior. If you are concerned about the HIV antibody results becoming part of your medical record, you can be tested through an anonymous test site or by using a home test kit. Check with your local or state public health department for more information about testing options.

What is an HIV test?

An HIV test determines whether someone has been infected by **human immunodeficiency virus (HIV)**, the virus that causes **acquired immunodeficiency syndrome (AIDS)**. You cannot obtain treatment for HIV infection unless you know if you are infected, and you cannot know if you are infected unless you take an HIV test.

How do I arrange to have an HIV test?

Thinking about getting an HIV test may be stressful because the result might be positive. But you need to know if you are infected by HIV in order to be able to control the disease. If the test shows that you are not HIV-infected, it will be an opportunity to plan ways to prevent becoming infected in the future. If you need help to overcome fears about getting an HIV test, there are many community organizations and hotlines that can provide you with information and support. You may wish to have someone accompany you when you go to have blood drawn for the HIV test and when you find out the results. If you are in recovery from drug use or are receiving mental health care, you may want to discuss the best time to be tested for HIV with a peer or counselor.

One reason many people fear having an HIV test performed is that they do not want others to know. If this is the case, you may want to consider anonymous testing. **Anonymous**

test sites (ATS) do not request any identifying information, such as your name or where you live. You are assigned a code number, and your blood specimen and test results are identified by that code only, so that no one except you can associate your name with your test result. There are ATS sites established in most major metropolitan areas, and you can find out their location by contacting your local HIV/AIDS service organization or hotline or department of public health. Test results are generally available in about two weeks. To get the results, you must have your code number with you. Anonymous testing is now also available through home kits. A sample of blood is placed on coded filter paper and sent to a testing laboratory. Results are obtained by calling a telephone number about one week later. If positive, a counselor will discuss the results with you and recommend local counseling and primary care services. Home testing kits, available at many pharmacies, cost between $45 and $55. They are generally not covered by health insurance.

Confidential test sites request information that identifies you, such as your name and medical record number. If you are tested through your doctor, the results will likely be included in your medical record. It is important to know that information recorded in your medical record may, with your permission, be reported to an insurance carrier. A court of law could also obtain your records in a legal case by issuing a subpoena. If these are potential concerns, you may want to be tested at an ATS or at home. However, you should understand that in order to receive medical care for HIV infection and be eligible for disability benefits, the test result must become part of your medical record.

What is HIV test counseling?

You should receive **counseling** as part of the HIV test procedure. Counseling means that a person will answer your questions and offer you general advice about the risks and benefits of the HIV test and about your particular concerns. All of your questions should be answered before taking the test, and you should feel free to change your mind at any time about being tested. If you think that an employer, insurance company, or court of law will request your HIV test result, take time to discuss with a counselor or friend what may happen if your test is positive. You may even choose to seek out legal advice concerning the situation.

You should be counseled after receiving your test result, whether it is negative or positive. If the test is negative, you should discuss ways to continue to prevent exposure to HIV and other sexually transmitted diseases. If the test is positive, ask questions. The testing site should be able to provide you with telephone numbers of HIV/AIDS service organizations and hotlines that can provide you with support and educational information. It is also very important to see a doctor, preferably one whom you already know. If you do not have one, ask for a referral to someone who has experience treating people with HIV infection. To determine the stage of HIV disease and the best strategy for treatment, your doctor will perform additional tests, such as a **CD4 cell ("T-cell") count** and **viral load**.

Remember, taking the HIV test is only the first step in dealing with HIV infection. Whether your test is positive or negative, there are many things that you can do to maintain good health. Effective therapies are now available to slow the progression of HIV disease, to treat and prevent complications, and to decrease its spread to others.

What does viral load mean?

Viral load (or viral burden) refers to a measurement of the number of HIV particles. The total viral load is the amount of HIV in your blood, lymph nodes, spleen, and other parts of your body. If your viral load measurement is high, it indicates that HIV is reproducing, and that the disease will likely progress faster than if your viral load is low.

What is viral load testing?

Viral load testing measures the number of HIV particles in your blood. These tests detect a kind of protein strand called RNA, which is a part of HIV containing the genes of the virus. Each HIV particle contains two copies of a molecule called RNA that carries the HIV genes. The viral load test determines the number of copies of HIV RNA molecules in a sample of blood.

Two laboratory techniques are generally used for viral load testing: **branched-chain DNA (bDNA)**, and **quantitative polymerase chain reaction (PCR)**. While the viral load test actually measures only the level of virus circulating in your blood, there is evidence that this value is a good indicator of the amount of virus in your entire body.

What do the results of a viral load test mean?

Viral load tests are reported as the number of HIV "copies" in a milliliter of blood. Results can generally be classified as high, low, and intermediate. General guidelines for understanding the results are as follows:

1) **High viral load:** greater than 30,000 (bDNA) or 55,000 (PCR) copies. This result indicates a higher risk for HIV disease progression. High viral load titers may range as high as one million copies or more.

2) **Low viral load:** less than 20 to 50 copies depending upon the assay used. This result indicates that HIV is not actively reproducing and that the risk of disease progression is low. It is important to realize that an "undetectable" test result does not mean that HIV infection is cured. Rather it indicates that the level of virus in the blood is lower than the test can measure.

Viral load results between these values (less than 30,000 [bDNA] to 55,000 [PCR] but greater than 20 to 50) are considered intermediate.

How is viral load testing helpful?

Your viral load test result provides important information that is used in conjunction with your **CD4 cell ("T-cell") count** to monitor the status of HIV disease, to guide recommendations for therapy, and to predict its future course. While the CD4 count is a marker of the health of your immune system (a high value is better), viral load testing directly measures the number of HIV particles circulating in your blood (a low value is better). **There is good evidence that keeping the viral load "as low as** possible for as long as possible" will decrease the likelihood of developing complications of HIV disease and will prolong life.

How is viral load testing used in managing HIV disease?

Doctors and researchers are still trying to determine how viral load testing should be best used for patient care. Most believe that viral load tests can be used to determine when to begin **antiretroviral (anti-HIV) therapy** and whether the drugs you are receiving are effective. **In general, antiretroviral therapy is recommended in persons with high viral loads especially if their CD4 count is below normal.** In persons with intermediate viral loads, either starting drug therapy or monitoring them off therapy may be reasonable options. If well tolerated, antiretroviral drugs are continued as long as they suppress the viral load.

When and how often should viral load testing be performed?

Baseline

Initially it is a good idea to have two viral load tests performed at separate visits. This will give a reliable measure of the baseline HIV level. If your viral load is low and CD4 count is normal, your doctor may not recommend antiretroviral therapy. If your viral load is high, your doctor will recommend that you start antiretroviral therapy.

Evaluating therapy

To determine if antiretroviral therapy is effective, you should have a viral load test performed along with a CD4 count about four weeks after starting therapy. In general, effective therapy should result in a significant drop in your viral load over this time period. This is defined as at least a factor of three-fold (for example, from 10,000 to less than 3,000). Your doctor will review the results with you and discuss the significance of the change in viral load.

Monitoring therapy

You should have a viral load test along with a CD4 count performed every three months to confirm that the antiretroviral drugs you are receiving continue to keep your viral level low.

To provide accurate comparisons, your doctor will send all the viral load tests to the same laboratory and have your blood samples analyzed by the identical technique. In general, viral loads should not be performed during a new illness or soon after a vaccination, as both of these

What is shingles?

Shingles, also called herpes zoster, is a treatable skin condition caused by **varicella-zoster virus** (VZV). An outbreak of shingles is characterized by a patch of skin becoming blistered and painful in a single area on one side of the body. VZV is also the cause of chickenpox.

How does one develop shingles?

All persons who have chickenpox during childhood are at risk of developing shingles in their adult life. After chickenpox resolves, the virus remains in an inactive state in the spinal nerve roots. With advancing age, especially if you have a condition such as HIV infection which impairs immune function, VZV can become activated, resulting in an outbreak of shingles. It is not understood exactly how the body controls whether VZV is active or inactive.

People with an active case of chickenpox develop blisters on their skin and have VZV in their blood and lung secretions. Through casual contact, they can easily spread the virus to others who have not had the infection. The virus is spread less easily through shingles lesions. The virus remains active until the lesions are dry and scabbed over, but direct contact is necessary to spread the virus to others. If you are HIV-infected and have not had chickenpox, it is best to avoid persons with active chickenpox and refrain from physical contact with those who have shingles. Through a blood test, your doctor can determine if you have had chicken pox in the past.

GETTING UNSTUCK

Girl to Girl, You can be, Infected indeed...
By Conscious

Published By:
SWN Publishing LLC
P.O. Box 1133
Union NJ, 07083-1133, USA
E-mail Conscious@prettytomboys.com

GETTING UNSTUCK is available at special discounts for bulk purchase, sales promotions, fundraising, or educational purposes. For details, Contact: Special Sales Department: SWN Publishing LLC, P.O. Box 1133, Union NJ, 07083-1133, USA.

ORDER FORM

Please send_____copy(ies) of Getting Unstuck to:

Name:_____
     First   MI   Last

Address:_____
     Street

_____
     City/State   Zip

Send check or money order for $17.95 per book plus $4.00 shipping and handling payable to:

SWN Publishing P.O. Box 1133 Union NJ, 07083-1133, USA

TAKE NOTES. WRITE YOUR FEELINGS DOWN